wine grape
press

THE CALIFORNIA WINEMAKERS COOK BOOK

Easy to prepare recipes specifically
created for the winemaker to
compliment your favorite California wines.

Edited by
Kenneth R. Parry

A Publication of the Wine Grape Press

The Wine Grape Press
A division of The Very Big Corporation
PO Box 151261
Lakewood, CO. 80215-1261
303.989.3338
303.986.1779 FAX
800.981.WINE

ISBN 1-886026-00-9

First printing August 1994

ACKNOWLEDGEMENTS

First of all, and most importantly, I'd like to thank all the wineries who generously contributed recipes for the book: their ability to place competitive concerns after their interest in educating the consumer is admirable and should be a lesson to those who didn't contribute about the power of non-competition; Alicia Parry, for her ability to recognize what can be, and undaunted, achieve what others dream as possible but are unwilling to assume the risks; Michael O' Dell, for not always believing in my hair-brained ideas but always believing in me; Eddy and Richard Clem at Sunset Printing for their printing assistance, without whom *The California Winemakers Cook Book* would not have been possible, <u>we are grateful</u>; Murry Huizingh, Joyce Boyd and everyone at Adam's Computers for their technical assistance and use of printing and scanning facilities; the Colorado retail wine merchants for sharing our interest in educating the consumer, sharing our love of wine, and their belief and support in this project and the Vintage Club; The Tattered Cover and Cook's Mart in Denver for their belief in the first book; all the wineries who bought the first book to sell in their tasting rooms; Vintage Club members who, without your support, this book would not have been possible and to the consumer for their seemingly insatiable interest in exploring wine with food: your passion is our motivator.

About The Cover...

Vanita Doyle is a native Californian who recently moved to Arvada from Texas. Her first love is oriental watercolors, but she also works in oils and acrylics. She has studied with a number of Oriental artists, but considers Diana Kan of New York to be her "Master."

Vanita has had work accepted in several annual Sumi-E Society of America's juried shows in New York and Washington D.C. While in Texas, she won many awards in shows in Houston and sold her work at shows throughout Texas and Louisiana. Vanita has exhibited and sold her work through many art shows and festivals since 1988 and she had her first one-woman show in Houston in 1992.

The cover art, entitled "Deep Purple", was first used as the poster for *Wines for Life*, a benefit wine tasting for the University of Colorado Cancer Center.

"Since most of my watercolor training has been in oriental techniques, I say my watercolors contain a 'touch of the orient' or some far eastern flair," says Vanita, "yet I consider my subject matter very contemporary. I give the paintings an oriental touch by painting mountains with mist and/or cloud, or by simplifying the subject matter."

We'd like to thank Vanita for use of this exquisite work for our cover.

Full color prints of the cover art, listing of future showings or other information are available through:

Vanita Doyle
303.425.7422

CONTENTS

| 9 | Old Fashioned Crab Cakes | |
| | BUENA VISTA | SAUVIGNON BLANC |

9 Old Fashioned Crab Cakes
    BUENA VISTA   SAUVIGNON BLANC

9 Lemon Chive Halibut
    SANFORD WINERY   SAUVIGNON BLANC

10 Cloved Lobster-Butter Canapes
    SANFORD WINERY   CHARDONNAY

10 Lemon Pepper Lobster
    SANFORD WINERY   CHARDONNAY

11 Oyster Flan with Fennel Fumet
    MIRASSOU   AU NATUREL CHAMPAGNE

12 New Potatoes with Smoked Salmon, Dill, and Yogurt
    FETZER VINEYARDS   CHARDONNAY

12 Scallop Quenelles
    RENAISSANCE VINEYARDS   DRY RIESLING

13 Rock Shrimp Radiatore
    BUENA VISTA WINERY   CHARDONNAY

Appetizer - Fruit

14 Spicy Apricot-Ginger Appetizer
    BANDIERA   WHITE ZINFANDEL

Appetizer - Meat

14 Beef Fillet on Mushrooms
    SANFORD WINERY   PINOT NOIR

15 Chicken Skewers
    PINE RIDGE   CHARDONNAY

16 Satay with Peanut Sauce
    CAKEBREAD CELLARS   SAUVIGNON BLANC

16 Sage Prosciutto Pork
    SANFORD WINERY   SAUVIGNON BLANC

Appetizer - Trout

27   Smoked Trout, Watercress, Pears and Fresh Dill on Belgian Endive Spears
        CAKEBREAD CELLARS   CHARDONNAY

Soups

29   Bean Soup
        OAK RIDGE VINEYARDS   FUME BLANC

29   Portuguese Soup
        HUSCH VINEYARDS   PINOT NOIR

30   Corn Chowder with Cumin and Red Pepper
        GROTH VINEYARDS & WINERY   SAUVIGNON BLANC

30   Fish Market Cioppino with Chardonnay
        SUTTER HOME   CHARDONNAY

31   Corn & Crayfish Soup
        EBERLE WINERY   CHARDONNAY

32   Cream of Green Lentil Soup
        IRON HORSE VINEYARDS   WEDDING CUVEE CHAMPAGNE

33   Minestone
        SEGHESIO WINERY   SANGIOVESE

34   Quick Minestrone
        SEBASTIANI VINEYARDS   CHARDONNAY

34   Chestnut Soup
        CAIN CELLARS   CAIN FIVE

35   Herb Vegetable Beef Soup
        SANFORD WINERY   PINOT NOIR-VIN GRIS

35   Chilled Curried Zucchini Soup
        RODNEY STRONG VINEYARDS   SAUVIGNON BLANC

36   Zucchini Soup
        GROTH VINEYARDS & WINERY   SAUVIGNON BLANC

Salads

Side Dish - Biscuits

Side Dish - Potato

Side Dish - Rice

Side Dish - Vegetables

Sauces

65	Pacific Salmon Chardonnay	
	BUENA VISTA WINERY	CHARDONNAY

66	Poached Salmon with Five Minute Sauces	
	KORBEL	CHAMPAGNE/BRUT

67	Seared Salmon with Rice Paper & a Citrus Vinaigrette	
	PEDRONCELLI	FUME BLANC

67	Scallops L'Orange	
	BYINGTON WINERY	FUME BLANC

68	Scallops with Papaya and Ginger Beurre Blanc	
	HUSCH VINEYARDS	CHARDONNAY

69	Sunshine Scallops	
	FOREST HILL VINEYARD	CHARDONNAY

69	Citrus & Apricot Prawns	
	HEITZ CELLAR	CHARDONNAY

70	Curried Crepe's filled with Sea Bass and Rock Prawns on a Merlot Beurre Rouge	
	CUVAISON	MERLOT

71	Fillet of Sole in Tarragon Orange Butter	
	DRY CREEK VINEYARDS	CHARDONNAY

72	Grilled Brook Trout with Pumpkin Sauce	
	FETZER VINEYARDS	CHARDONNAY

73	Walnut Encrusted Trout	
	SHAFER VINEYARDS	CHARDONNAY

Main Course - Meat/Beef

74	Filets with Groth Cabernet	
	GROTH VINEYARDS & WINERY	CABERNET SAUVIGNON

74	Flank Steak Extraordinaire	
	ST. SUPERY	CABERNET SAUVIGNON

| 84 | Italian Chicken | |
| | SEGHESIO WINERY | SAUVIGNON BLANC |

| 85 | Parmesan Walnut Chicken with Mustard Sauce | |
| | DRY CREEK VINEYARDS | FUME BLANC |

| 85 | Roast Chicken Royal | |
| | OAK RIDGE VINEYARDS | WHITE ZINFANDEL |

| 86 | Roast Chicken with Lemon and Olives | |
| | IRON HORSE VINEYARDS | PINOT NOIR |

| 87 | Roasted Chicken | |
| | FROG'S LEAP | CHARDONNAY |

| 88 | Sa-Teh on Skewers | |
| | PINE RIDGE | CHENIN BLANC |

| 89 | Steamed Chicken Breasts Stuffed with Red Pepper Mousse in Champagne Sauce | |
| | MIRASSOU | BRUT CHAMPAGNE |

| 90 | Thai Grilled Chicken | |
| | MURPHY-GOODE WINERY | SAUVIGNON BLANC |

Main Course - Meat/Duck

| 90 | Dijon Duck Breasts | |
| | SANFORD WINERY | PINOT NOIR |

| 92 | Roast Duckling with Green Peppercorn Sauce | |
| | RENAISSANCE VINEYARDS | CABERNET SAUVIGNON |

Main Course - Meat/Game Hen

| 93 | Grappa and Wine Marinated Cornish Game Hen | |
| | CA' DEL SOLO | PRUNUS |

| 93 | Roasted Cornish Game Hens | |
| | LOUIS M. MARTINI WINERY | GEWURZTRAMINER |

Main Course - Meat/Lamb

| 94 | Barbequed Leg of Lamb | |
| | HEITZ CELLARS | CABERNET SAUVIGNON |

Main Course - Meat/Pork

Main Course Meat/Quail

Main Course - Meat/Sausage

Main Course - Meat/Veal

103   Escalopes de Veau au Chanterelle
       BYINGTON WINERY   PINOT NOIR

104   Ficklin Port Marinated Roast Loin of Veal
       FICKLIN VINEYARDS   TINTA PORT

105   Porcini Veal Stew
       CHALK HILL WINERY   CABERNET SAUVIGNON

105   Vin Gris Veal Chops
       SANFORD WINERY   PINOT NOIR-VIN GRIS

Main Course - Pasta

106   Clam Pasta
       LOUIS M. MARTINI WINERY   CHARDONNAY

106   Lasagna with Besciamella Sauce
       SEGHESIO WINERY   ZINFANDEL

107   Pasta with Italian Sausage & Zinfandel
       SUTTER HOME   ZINFANDEL

108   Pasta with Scallops in Lemon Herb-Cream Sauce
       MC DOWELL VALLEY VINEYARDS   FUME' BLANC

109   Pasta with Shrimp, Asparagus and Cream Sauce
       CHALK HILL WINERY   SAUVIGNON BLANC

109   Penne Puttanesca
       SEGHESIO WINERY   ZINFANDEL

110   Saffron Pasta Fettuccini with Duck Confit and Crimini Mushrooms
       THE HESS COLLECTION   CABERNET SAUVIGNON

111   Won Ton Ravioli with Paprika Cream
       CLOS PEGASE   CHARDONNAY

Main Course - Pizza

112   Pizza with Roast Eggplant, Peppers, Red Onions & Fresh Herbs
       CAKEBREAD CELLARS   CABERNET SAUVIGNON

Dessert - Cake

Dessert - Chocolate

Dessert - Cookies

Dessert - Fruit

Dessert- Macaroons

"Wine is constant proof that God loves us and loves to see us happy."

-Benjamin Franklin

"Wine rejoices the heart of man, and Joy is the mother of all virtue."

-Goethe

"To eat is human, to digest, divine."
-Mark Twain

"I feast on wine and bread,
and feasts they are."

-Michelangelo

WELCOME TO WINE WITH FOOD:
THE CALIFORNIA WINEMAKERS COOK BOOK

Over the years, the question most frequently asked by wine drinkers at wine tastings has always been, "What food would you recommend with 'this' wine?" The question fortunately or unfortunately has no specifically correct answer, because all cabernets and all chardonnays are not created equal. Different regions, different valleys, even the different slopes the vines were grown on all have a hand in creating the delicate nuances of the wine. And the ideal food would compliment the individual delicacies of each individual wine. Sure, there are always the pat answers: cabernet with red meat or chocolate; chardonnay with lobster, but such generalities do nothing to enhance the specific characteristics of a wine. And when the wine compliments the food, the entire meal is enhanced as the individual character of each is released and becomes recognizable. This book was begun with this dilemma in mind: How to answer this most perplexing question, What food would you recommend with 'this' wine?

Winemakers, from the smallest to the largest wineries, tour the country sharing their love of wine and their philosophy through winemaker dinners. The wineries go to great lengths (and great expense in some cases) to create dishes that will bring out the delicate characteristics of their wine (many times they hire internationally renowned chefs to specifically create dishes for their wines). Since the wineries have invested so much time and effort to develop recipes which compliment your wines, their assistance was invaluable in creating this book.

270 of California's most respected wineries were asked to submit recipes from their winemaker dinners or in the tasting rooms for our book. We asked the wineries to put away their competitive concerns momentarily and consider the overall benefit to the wine industry by educating the consumer about the remarkable marriage between wine and food. Most everyone we spoke with were enthusiastic about the project and more than willing to participate. For the sake of credibility, we did not ask wineries for remuneration for their recipes to be included in the book though many offered. <u>The book was made available to any winery who wished to participate.</u>

The *California Winemakers Cook Book* contains a potpourri of winemakers favorite recipes created to compliment their wines. With this book, we want to encourage consumers to try the wines with the food they go best with. (What better way to 'discover' a wine then with the dish that best compliments its character.) Most wineries submitted recipes designed to compliment their wines as a beverage, but others provided recipes designed with the wine as an essential ingredient. It seems to us either method accomplishes the same goal: enjoyment of wine with food.

Most pages feature the recipe and the specific wine label (or winery logo) for easy consumer recognition. The book covers appetizers, soups, salads, side dishes, sauces, entrees and desserts, and each category is indexed by type of food (meat, fish, pasta) in the table of contents. At the end of the book, under appendix A & B, the recipes are listed by wine type and by winery. Here the reader will be able to locate all the recipes for a given varietal in the book, and hopefully notice the diversity of the dishes created for the wines. Further, the recipes run from the sublime to the exotic, from Bean Soup to Wild Boar Ribs, again to encourage diversity.

The recipes were created with the style of wine in mind, to compliment a particular wine, but you'll soon discover that other winerys wines will produce the same enjoyment (if a dish was created to compliment a cabernet sauvignon, it goes to follow that the dish will compliment many cabernets). Don't be afraid to experiment and try the recipes you enjoy with other wines.

Some wineries submitted actual winemaker dinners intact: multiple recipes designed to be served as an entire meal.

Mirassou sent in "A Sparkling Menu" for the holidays designed around three courses and an simple salad, all created by Mirassou's Chef, Felix Talavan. The meal consists of the recipes Oyster Flan (p.11), Steamed Chicken Breasts (p.89), and Brandied Cranberry Cake (p. 116). These recipes, combined with buttered green beans, rice pilaf, and a salad of butter lettuce with toasted walnuts make for a wonderful meal for Champagnes (or sparkling wines).

Pine Ridge submitted their "Spring Luncheon", a complete six course meal for chardonnay consisting of Skewered Tortellini (p.23), Chicken Skewers (p.15), Honey Roasted Pork (p.99), Lacy Potato Pancakes (p.49), Tarragon-Orange Vinaigrette (p.39), and Olive Oil Cake (p.120).

Renaissance Winery presents in a six course menu consisting of Roast Duckling (p.92), Scallops Quenelles (p.12), Pasta with Lobster Sauce (p. 63), Arroz con Pollo (p.79), Pear Pie (p.124), and Almond Biscotti (p.114).

Bonny Doon Vineyards sent in a grappa trio, including appetizer, entree and dessert. Bonny Doon produces products under a few different labels including the Ca' del Solo brand (two of the three wines are Ca' del Solo). Grappas are "fortified" wines infused with brandy. Randall Grahm, owner and winemaker at Bonny Doon, is renowned for creating some of the most unusual and yet remarkable wines avail able. Try this trio for a most unusual taste treat.

We've tried to make this book as easy to use as possible. We attempted to standardize abbreviations within recipes: T. =Tablespoon, t. =teaspoon, C. =cup, but did not attempt to justify the sometimes ambiguous term "done", we'll leave that up to the reader. All recipe notes have been left intact and are in the authors first-person narrative.

Remember to keep an open mind when using this book as our intent was to foster experimentation. If you know the winery and are unfamiliar with the meal, or if your love the meal but haven't heard of the wine, try it; *take a chance.*

You'll discover more hidden treasures between these pages than you thought imaginable. A whole new world of Wine with Food possibilities exist. Whether you're new to wine or an experienced connoisseur, some culinary delights await you.

Bon Appetit!

Ken Parry
June 1994

Appetizers

SANFORD WINERY
PINOT NOIR-VIN GRIS

Lemon Sun Tomatoes Crostini
Created especially by Shirley Sarvis to serve with Sanford Pinot Noir-Vin Gris.

About 10 slices non-sour baguette slices, (each about 2 by 1-1/2 inches), 1/4 inch thick
Light very fresh olive oil (preferably Olio Sasso pure olive oil)
1-1/2 T. very finest short slivers of drained quality sun-dried tomatoes (preferably Vail 'Aurea, Ardoino brand)
1-1/2 t. freshly grated fresh lemon peel
1/2 C. finest julienne of fresh young tender spinach leaves (no stems) which have been washed and dried (gather leaves together to cut the fine chiffonade)

Freshly ground premium quality black pepper (such as Panapee or Malibar). Brush each baguette slice generously with olive oil on both sides. Broil-toast until light golden (no browner, with no overbrown edges) on both sides and crisp throughout; place on rack to cool and crisp. Gently and thoroughly turn together tomato, lemon peel, spinach and enough oil to cloak well (about 1 teaspoon). Pile loosely and deeply and neatly onto each toast slice. Add a light grinding of black pepper. Serve immediately. Makes about 10 appetizers.

KENWOOD VINEYARDS
CABERNET SAUVIGNON

Sun Dried Tomato Crostini with Asiago Cheese

Crostini:
1 baguette, 1/4" sliced (24 slices)
1/4 C. olive oil
2 t. sweet butter
2 cloves garlic, minced

Preheat oven to 350°. Heat olive oil, butter and garlic until the butter is melted. Brush the oil-butter mixture on both sides of the bread slices and place on a baking sheet. Cook until a golden brown.

Sun Dried Tomato Paste:
1 8 oz. jar sun dried tomatoes in olive oil. Process until a paste.
Asiago cheese, 1/3 lb. crumbled

Continued...

To assemble: Spread a Tbsp of paste on each crostini. Toast the crostini and top with Asiago cheese. Bake until cheese is melted. Serve with Kenwood Sonoma Valley or Jack London Vineyard Cabernet Sauvignon.

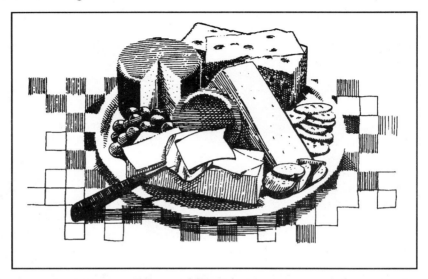

RODNEY STRONG VINEYARDS
PINOT NOIR

Chever Cheese & Roasted Walnuts
Recipe courtesy of John Ash

1/3 C. Walnuts, roasted in oven at 350° for 5 minutes
1/2 C. Walnut oil
1 T. Red wine vinegar
1 clove sliced garlic (remove before serving)
1/2 t. Salt
Ground pepper

Mix together. Allow to steep 3-4 hours. Spoon over a slice of Chevre (goat cheese) on baby lettuce leaves.

BONNY DOON VINEYARDS
GRAPPA DI MOSCATO

Bonny Doon Vineyard

Grappa Marinated Goat Cheese

Marinate overnight , a 6-8 oz. portion of fresh mild goat cheese in a large enough bowl to accommodate:
2-3 T. extra virgin olive oil
1 clove garlic, minced
1/8 t. tobasco sauce
2 T. Bonny Doon Grappa di Moscato or Niagara
2 T. fresh parsley, chopped

Cover and refrigerate 8 to 48 hours, remove from refrigerator about 2 hours prior to serving. Serve with a baguette sliced thin and toasted. Serves 4 to 8 as an hors d'oeuvre.

PINE RIDGE
MERLOT

PINE RIDGE WINERY

Grilled Eggplant and Cheese Appetizer
Serves 6-8

1 eggplant, sliced 3/4" thick
1 C. tomato sauce
1 T. fresh oregano, chopped
1 T. olive oil
salt to taste
pepper to taste

3 tomatoes, peeled, seeded, and diced
1/4 C. balsamic vinegar
4 large slices Jack or Mozzarella
1 red onion, sliced 1/2" thick

Sprinkle eggplant with salt and let sit for 1/2-hour. Pat dry after rinsing. Grill or sauté until just cooked through, set aside and keep warm. Add together tomatoes, tomato sauce, oregano, olive oil, salt and pepper, to taste. Set aside.

Grill or sauté red onion until just cooked. Slightly separate rings and sprinkle with balsamic vinegar until lightly coated. In oven proof pan, place 1/2 tomato mixture, put eggplant and onion rings on top in circular pattern, cover with slices of cheese. Bake in 375° oven until cheese melts. Warm the remaining tomato mixture.

Serve slices of baked eggplant with remaining warm tomato sauce over top.

SUTTER HOME
WHITE ZINFANDEL

Onion & Cheese Appetizers with White Zinfandel

3 green onions, minced
1/2 C. fresh parmesan cheese, grated
1/4 C. Sutter Home White Zinfandel
1/4 C. mayonnaise
2 T. sliced pimento, drained
1 clove garlic (optional), pressed or minced
1 long baguette (1 lb.) cut into 18-1/4" thick slices

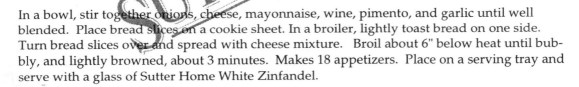

In a bowl, stir together onions, cheese, mayonnaise, wine, pimento, and garlic until well blended. Place bread slices on a cookie sheet. In a broiler, lightly toast bread on one side. Turn bread slices over and spread with cheese mixture. Broil about 6" below heat until bubbly, and lightly browned, about 3 minutes. Makes 18 appetizers. Place on a serving tray and serve with a glass of Sutter Home White Zinfandel.

GROTH VINEYARDS & WINERY
SAUVIGNON BLANC

Groth

1991
Napa Valley
Sauvignon Blanc

PRODUCED AND BOTTLED BY
GROTH VINEYARDS & WINERY, OAKVILLE, CALIFORNIA, USA
ALCOHOL 13 % BY VOLUME

Pesto Cheese Hors d'oeuvre

Pesto:
3-1/2 C. fresh basil leaves
1-1/2 C. parmesan cheese
3/4 C. olive oil
4 cloves garlic, crushed
1/4 C. pine nuts
salt and pepper to taste

Cheese:
1-1/2 lbs. cream cheese
1 lb. butter
1 C. parmesan cheese

Blend the cheese until smooth. The pesto is most easily prepared in a food processor or blender. The herbs etc. should be blended until well mixed. To prepare the mold, use a 10 cup container, loaf pan or Charlotte mold. Line the pan with 2 layers of dampened cheese cloth. Make two alternating layers of cheese and pesto, then fold the cheese cloth layers over the top. When the cheese is firm, remove from mold and cheese cloth. Wrap in plastic wrap until served. Serve with a baguette or fresh vegetables and Groth Sauvignon Blanc.

CAKEBREAD CELLARS
CHARDONNAY

Suppli Telephono
Serves 8

Cakebread Cellars

1/2 onion, chopped
1 clove garlic, minced
2 T. olive oil
1 C. arborio rice
1/2 C. pumpkin, grated
32 oz. chicken stock, preferably homemade

1/4 C. parmesan cheese, grated
1 C. mozzarella, grated
1 egg
bread crumbs
peanut oil for frying

Place the chicken stock on the back of the stove and keep at a simmer. In a heavy bottom saucepan sauté onion and garlic in olive oil til soft. Add rice and toss to coat. Add a ladle of chicken stock and stir until it is absorbed. Repeat this procedure, adding a ladle of chicken stock and stirring until it is absorbed. Add the pumpkin half way through the cooking process after about 10 minutes. Rice is done when it is still "al dente" like pasta, about 25-30 minutes. Remove from heat and allow to cool. Stir in cheese and egg. Refrigerate to chill, about an hour. Form into balls and roll in bread crumbs.

Heat enough peanut oil to cover rissono balls by 2 inches on top of the stove to 350°. Use a wide pan with high sides, oil will bubble up as balls cook. Fry in small batches until golden. 2-3 minutes. Remove to paper towels to absorb excess oil. Transfer to serving trays and serve warm with a glass of Cakebread Cellars Chardonnay Reserve.

Note: If these are pulled apart while still hot the cheese forms strings, hence the name "Telephone Wires".

SEGHESIO WINERY
SAUVIGNON BLANC

Torte

"I first made this recipe when a young man from Switzerland, Pierre Sauty, lived with us. He wanted to learn how winery and viticultural practices in California differed from his own country. He now has his own winery and vineyards near Lake Geneva. He especially liked this and I have been making it ever since."

3 leeks
1 bundle chard
1 C. cooked rice
1 C. grated Gruyere cheese
2/3 C. Romano cheese
3 or 4 eggs, beaten
1 C. fresh dried bread crumbs

Trim the roots and remove any withered leaves of the leeks. Wash thoroughly and chop. Cut the center stalk out of the chard - rinse several times. Chop leaves of chard and then sauté leeks and chard in olive oil and butter until they cook down, allow to cool. Then mix this with the cooked rice, Gruyere and Romano cheese. Add the eggs and stir in the bread crumbs. Put it into a greased 7-1/2 x 12 inch Pyrex dish. It may be made with a baked crust and cooked in a pie dish. Bake in a 350° oven for about 40 minutes. Remove and let cool. Cut into 1 x 2 inch size squares or slice if baked in a pie dish.

This Torte is tasty prepared as either an hors d'oeuvre or vegetable dish. Our guests seem to enjoy it either way. Mangiamo!

CAKEBREAD CELLARS
CHARDONNAY

Miniature Crab Cakes with Homemade Tartar Sauce
Serves 5

1/2 lb. crab meat, cleaned
1/2 C. mayonnaise, preferably homemade
1/4 C. celery, minced
2 T. shallots, minced
2 T. Dijon mustard
squeeze of lemon
dash of cayenne
2 T. bread crumbs

1 C. flour, sifted
2 eggs, beaten with 2 T. water
2 C. bread crumbs - dried
peanut oil for frying

Cakebread Cellars

Pick through crab meat thoroughly to make sure that it is free of shells. Combine the next 6 ingredients. Add just enough bread crumbs to tighten the mixture up and taste for seasoning. Adjust as necessary.

Form into small balls and roll in flour to coat, followed by egg and finally the bread crumbs. Place on a sheet tray and refrigerate until ready to use.

At the last moment drop into hot peanut oil (350°) and fry until golden brown. Remove to a sheet of paper towels and transfer to a serving tray. Serve warm with tartar sauce and a glass of Cakebread Cellars Chardonnay.

Homemade Tartar Sauce:

1/2 C. mayonnaise, preferably homemade
1 T. celery, minced
1 T. shallots, minced
2 T. pickle relish

1 t. capers, chopped
1 t. Dijon mustard
1 T. parsley, chopped
2-3 dashes tabasco

Combine all of the above ingredients and taste for seasoning. Adjust accordingly.

SANFORD WINERY
CHARDONNAY

SANFORD

Chervil Lobster in Lettuce
Created especially by Shirley Sarvis to serve with Sanford Chardonnay.

1/2 lb. lightly poached or steamed fresh Maine lobster meat, cut into 1/4 inch chunks
white pepper dressing (recipe follows)
about 24 small inner heart (about 2") leaves of fresh limestone lettuce (or tender butter)
Fresh chervil to garnish

Gently turn lobster with enough dressing to cloak rather generously. Salt and pepper to taste. Pile lightly into lettuce cups to fill generously. Garnish each at side-top with a small feather of chervil. Arrange on serving tray. Makes about 24 appetizers.

White Pepper Dressing:
3/8 t. salt
1 T. fresh lemon juice

1/4 t. white pepper, freshly ground
1/3 C. heavy whipping cream

Combine above ingredients. Beat with a whisk until mixture is foamy and creamy, about 30 seconds. Gradually beat in 2 T. very light olive oil. Fold in enough finely snipped fresh chervil leaves to season lightly, about 4 tsp.

BUENA VISTA WINERY
CHARDONNAY

Smoked Salmon Paté

1/2 lb. hot smoked salmon, chunked
1 T. extra virgin olive oil
8 oz. cream cheese, cut into pieces
1/4 C. Buena Vista Carneros Chardonnay
1 T. fresh lemon juice

3 green onions, chopped
2 T. fresh dill, chopped

Place cream cheese in bowl of food processor. Pulse 2-3 times until creamy. Add salmon chunks. Pulse until cream cheese and salmon are well mixed. Slowly add remaining ingredients while food processor is running. Transfer to a serving dish, cover and chill two hours or overnight. Remove paté from the refrigerator one hour before serving.

BUENA VISTA
SAUVIGNON BLANC

Old Fashioned Crab Cakes

1 lb. crab meat
1 small onion, diced
2 ribs celery, diced
1 red pepper, diced
1/2 C. flour
2 eggs
1/2 C. chopped parsley
juice of one lemon
salt and pepper to taste

Combine all ingredients in a bowl. Form into cakes (about a 1/2 cup). Fry in a small amount of oil or butter until golden brown on both sides. Serve at once with tartar sauce, or roasted pepper mayonnaise or any appropriate sauce. Serve with Buena Vista Lake County Sauvignon Blanc.

SANFORD WINERY
SAUVIGNON BLANC

Lemon Chive Halibut

Created especially by Shirley Sarvis to serve with Sanford Sauvignon Blanc. Good accompaniments: buttered fresh green beans, lightly seasoned with dry basil, and crispy crusted, non-sour French bread. Perhaps follow with a butter-lettuce salad with light oil-vinegar dressing. For dessert: fresh ripe plums, or persimmon-almond pudding or cinnamon cobbler with whipped cream.

4-6 oz. pieces of fresh, skinless fillet of halibut
salt and freshly ground pepper
2 T. grated fresh lemon peel

3 T. chives, snipped
5 T. butter

Wipe fish dry. Season well with salt and pepper. Arrange in a single layer in a shallow baking pan. Sprinkle with lemon peel and chives; dot with butter. Bake in a 350° oven until fish is opaque almost to center, about 10 to 12 minutes. Baste occasionally. Lift to serving plates. Spoon juices over. Makes 4 servings.

9

SANFORD WINERY
CHARDONNAY

Cloved Lobster-Butter Canapes

Created especially by Shirley Sarvis. Taste carefully as you season the lobster butter; you want only enough clove to give the slightest taste, not enough to cover the taste of the lobster. Arrange canapes on serving platters. Garnish, if you wish, with fresh celery leaves (this garnish is for presentation only and not to be eaten with this wine).

1/2 C. (4 ounces) soft unsalted butter
4 oz. lightly poached or steamed and cooled fresh Maine lobster prime meat, finely diced
Salt
Fresh coarsely ground black pepper
1/8 t. ground cloves
1-1/2 inch rounds of very thinly sliced, excellent non-sour French style bread, crusts removed, lightly buttered

Stir together butter, lobster, salt and pepper to season generously, and cloves. Pile deeply and loosely on bread rounds. Center each with a fresh grinding of black pepper. Makes about 20 appetizers.

SANFORD WINERY
CHARDONNAY

Lemon Pepper Lobster

1/2 lb lightly poached or steamed impeccably fresh Maine Lobster prime meat (freshly cooked and slightly warm or cooled just to room temperature)
1/4 C. warm clarified unsalted butter
1 t. grated fresh lemon peel
1/4 t. fresh finely ground premium white pepper

Cut lobster into attractive bite-sized (about one-inch) pieces. Arrange in an mound on serving platter. Have available at side, small lobster forks or small bamboo skewers. Stir together butter, lemon peel, pepper, and salt to taste. Offer butter in small pot or cup placed at side of lobster and set over a small flame to keep warm. Guests lift lobster morsel with fork and dip it into the butter to cloak well. Makes about 36 appetizers.

MIRASSOU
AU NATUREL CHAMPAGNE

Oyster Flan with Fennel Fumet

Fennel Fumet:
4 cups chicken stock, unsalted
2 T. fennel seeds
salt & pepper to taste

Combine stock and fennel seeds in a saucepan. Bring to a boil, lower heat, and simmer for 30 minutes. Strain out fennel seeds and season to taste with salt and white pepper.

Oyster Flan:
6 small (4-6 oz.) souffle molds (or oven-proof cups, well buttered)
12 shucked oysters with juice
4 T. unsalted butter
1/2 large onion, chopped
1/2 T. fennel seeds
1-1/2 C. heavy cream
2 eggs
salt and white pepper to taste
2 T. chives, chopped
2 oz. Salmon caviar (optional)

Place oysters with their juice in a small saucepan. Simmer gently just until oysters become opaque (about 1-2 minutes). Drain oysters in a sieve, reserving all the juice. Melt butter in a saucepan over medium heat. Add onions and fennel seeds. Cook slowly until onion is translucent but not browned. Add cream and oyster juice. Increase heat to medium-high and boil until cream is reduced to one cup. Strain. Whisk eggs in a bowl, then slowly whisk in hot cream. Season custard with salt and pepper. Place two oysters in each mold and divide custard among molds. Place molds in a roasting pan. Add water to come 2/3 up the sides of the molds. Bake in pre-heated oven at 325° for 35 minutes or until well set.

Allow to cool slightly. Run a knife tip around the sides of each mold. Reheat fennel fumet. Unmold each oyster flan into the middle of a heated, shallow soup plate. Pour in some fennel fumet and sprinkle with chopped chives.

Optional: *Garnish the top of each flan with a spoonful of salmon caviar. Serve with Mirassou Au Naturel Champagne.*

FETZER VINEYARDS
CHARDONNAY

New Potatoes with Smoked Salmon, Dill, and Yogurt

24 small new potatoes (half-dollar size)
1-1/4 C. plain yogurt
4 T. scallions, minced
2 T. capers, drained and minced
1/3 C. fresh dill, minced
1/3 lb. thinly sliced smoked salmon, cut into wide strips

Cook potatoes in lightly salted boiling water or in microwave until just done. Be careful not to overcook. Cool in cold water, pat dry, and scoop out center, leaving 1/4" cup. Carefully shave bottoms of potatoes so they don't tip over. Mix yogurt, scallions, capers, and dill together and spoon into potatoes. Arrange salmon strips attractively over top and garnish with ground pepper and dill sprigs.

RENAISSANCE VINEYARDS
DRY RIESLING

Scallop Quenelles

Panade:
1/2 cup cream
salt, white pepper
1 T. sweet butter
1/2 T. sweet butter

Heat cream and butter in saucepan until pot boils. Immediately add the flour, stirring quickly to blend. Season with salt and pepper. Chill.

In cuisinart, puree the chilled panade and gradually add:
1/2 of 16 fresh scallops
4 oz. sweet butter
1 egg and 1 egg yolk

Continued...

12

Salt, white pepper, nutmeg to taste

Check seasonings by cooking a small spoonful dropped into simmering water. It floats when cooked. Chill mixture until firm.

On a well-floured surface roll spoonfuls of the chilled mixture into 2" cylinders, fatter at the center with tapered ends (like baby cigars). Makes about 20. Place on a floured tray and chill. Bring a pot of water to a simmer and poach the quenelles; when they float, remove with a slotted spoon and place in a buttered baking pan, not touching. Chill.

Meanwhile prepare the sauce:

2 shallots, minced
2-3 cloves garlic, minced
2 T. butter

1/2 - 3/4 bottle of Renaissance Dry Riesling
2 C. cream
thyme, cayenne, salt to taste

Sauté the shallots and garlic in the batter until about 1/2; add the cream and reduce until slightly thickened. Twenty minutes before serving, ladle 2/3 of the sauce over the chilled quenelles and bake for 20 minutes in a preheated 350°oven. Quenelles will puff and should be served immediately: two each, with a little extra spooned on top. Garnish with a little lemon zest and chives.

BUENA VISTA CHARDONNAY

Since 1857

Buena Vista

W I N E R Y

Rock Shrimp Radiatore

8 oz. rock shrimp devained
1 T. olive oil
1 shallot, diced
2 cloves garlic, diced
2 Roma tomatoes, chopped
1 roasted red bell pepper, chopped

1/2 C. Buena Vista Carneros Chardonnay
pinch of saffron
2 C. blanched radiatore pasta
2 t. butter
juice of 1/2 a lemon

Sauté shrimp in hot skillet in olive oil. Add shallot, garlic, tomato, red pepper and sauté 30 seconds. Add 1/2 cup chardonnay and 5 capers and saffron. Reduce to half. Add 2 cups pasta and salt and pepper to taste. Add 2 tsp. butter to finish and lemon juice. Top with fresh herbs and parmesan cheese. Serve with Buena Vista Carneros Chardonnay.

BANDIERA
WHITE ZINFANDEL

Spicy Apricot-Ginger Appetizer

1 small jar apricot preserves
2 T. fresh ginger, peeled and chopped
1 t. red pepper flakes
1 - 8 oz. package cream cheese
1 package crackers

Combine apricot, ginger and red pepperflakes in a
small mixing bowl. Unwrap cream cheese and place on serving dish. Spoon apricot mixture
over cream cheese and serve with crackers. Perfect picnic addition when served with
Bandiera White Zinfandel!

SANFORD WINERY
PINOT NOIR

Beef Fillet on Mushrooms
Created especially by Shirley Sarvis.

1-1/2 lb. length of aged beef tenderloin, trimmed of fat, room temp.
salt and freshly ground black pepper
1-1/2 T. butter
golden sautéd mushrooms (recipe follows)
Very thin slices of crispy, crusted non-sour French bread baguettes

Wipe meat dry. Rub surface with salt and pepper to season well. Cloak with about 2 tsp.
melted, cooled butter. Let stand 1 hr. Place on rack in shallow roasting pan and bake in a
500° oven until very rare (meat thermometer at 115° to 120° at thickest part of fillet; temperature will rise upon resting; begin checking at about 13 minutes). Prepare each appetizer just
before serving to each quest: lift a thick layering of mushrooms to a baguette slice. Carve
beef very thinly across the grain; place one or two slices, in a rich ripple, on top of mushrooms. Sprinkle with more salt and pepper if needed. Makes about 18 appetizers

Golden sautéd Mushrooms:
1/3 C. unsalted butter
1 lb. fresh mushrooms, thinly sliced

Continued...

Heat butter in a heavy frying pan over medium-high heat until it bubbles. Add mushrooms and sauté, gently stirring frequently, until all mushroom liquid disappears and mushrooms are deep golden brown and edged with toastiness and generously cloaked with butter. Season with salt as necessary.

PINE RIDGE CHARDONNAY

PINE RIDGE WINERY

Chicken Skewers
Makes 20 skewers

1-1/2 lb. boneless, skinless chicken breast
1/3 C. white OR red wine
1/4 C. olive oil
3 hard green OR red apples, cut into 1" chunks

1 T. Balsamic OR red wine vinegar
1/2 C. chopped chutney

Cut the chicken into 3/4-inch cubes. Put in a large mixing bowl. Add the vinegar, wine, chutney, and olive oil and stir to combine. Marinate for at least 4 hours, or overnight. Drain the chicken and put on small, 6-inch skewers alternating with apple chunks. Broil or grill over hot coals for 8 - 10 minutes. Serve hot.

Variations: *Chicken can also be skewered with colored bell pepper squares, green onions, pineapple chunks, whole mushrooms, or pieces of celery.*

CAKEBREAD CELLARS
SAUVIGNON BLANC

Cakebread Cellars

Satay with Peanut Sauce

The recipes for this hors d'oeuvre came from two well known authorities on the cuisine of Asia, Bruce Cost and Hugh Carpenter. The marinade comes from Bruce Cost's Asian ingredients: *Buying and Cooking the Staple Foods of China, Japan and Southeast Asia*. The sauce is from *Chopstix* by Hugh Carpenter.

1 lb. chicken breasts or large shrimp
1 package bamboo skewers (soak in water the night before)

Marinade:

2 cloves garlic, minced	2 T. brown sugar
2 t. coriander (toasted & ground)	2 T. fish sauce
2 t. curnin (toasted & ground)	2 T. peanut oil

6 T. tamarind water (soak a small ball of pulp in 1/4 C. hot water to soften and pass through a strainer)

Remove skin from chicken breasts and discard. Cut into small strips and place in a small mixing bowl. If using shrimp, shell and de-vein and place in a bowl.

Mix together marinade ingredients and pour over chicken or shrimp. Allow to marinate for at least an hour. Then thread onto the end of the bamboo skewers and grill over a very hot fire. Serve with a small dish of Satay Sauce and a glass of Cakebread Cellars Sauvignon Blanc.

SANFORD WINERY
SAUVIGNON BLANC

SANFORD

Sage Prosciutto Pork

Created especially by Shirley Sarvis to serve with Sanford Sauvignon Blanc, this prosciutto will cling to the pork as the skewer is lifted to be eaten. Garnish serving trays with fresh sage leaves. The prosciutto should be lean, mild, moist, and fully spiced, not salty nor dry seeming. This subdued character is important in order that the prosciutto taste will be gentle toward the wine and will show the taste of the sage.

1 lb fresh boneless pork loin which has been completely trimmed of fat

Continued...

16

Salt and freshly ground black pepper
2-1/2 T. minced fresh sage OR 4 t. ground dry sage
Small amount of very clean and light tasting olive or other salad oil
2 oz. thinly sliced lean, moist, and somewhat mild prosciutto, cut into fine julienne strips

Very thinly, slice pork across the grain. Place single layer of slices between two sheets of waxed paper, and pat with a meat pounder or rolling pin to thinness, about 1/8 inch thick. Cut each slice, lengthwise, into strips about 1-1/4 inches wide. Season with salt and generously with pepper, and with the sage. Cover with waxed paper or clear plastic wrap and let stand for 1 hour if possible.

Thread on small skewers (and spread to be nearly flat) to make individual appetizers; brush both sides very lightly with oil. Place on a hot grill (or large heavy frying pan placed over high heat until hot) and grill to be golden brown on the outside and lush and juicy on the inside (not at all charred). Arrange on serving platter. Sprinkle with prosciutto, serve hot. Makes about 48 finger-food appetizers.

IRON HORSE VINEYARDS
FUME BLANC

Rabbit Sausage

2 rabbits, boneless (approximately 4 pounds)   2 C. heavy cream
1 -1/4 lbs. bacon   2 t. salt
1 leek, white part only, finely diced   2 t. fresh grated nutmeg
1/2 C. Iron Horse Fume Blanc   1 T. fresh thyme leaves
1/2 C. fresh bread crumbs   1/2 t. ground white pepper
2 T. unsalted butter   1/2 t. cayenne

Heat the butter in a large skillet. Add the onions and soften but do not brown; add the wine. Cook approximately 5 minutes over medium heat allowing the wine to evaporate. Set onions aside. Put the bread crumbs in a bowl, add half the cream, and allow bread to soak. Cut the rabbit and bacon into cubes and grind through a meat grinder using a medium size plate. Mix ground rabbit mixture with the onions, cream and bread crumbs, blending well. Pull through the meat grinder two more times to achieve a mousse-like consistency. Add the rest of the cream and seasonings. Mix well and form into patties.

To cook, place on grill over medium heat coals. Cook 4 to 5 minutes on each side. Serve with Iron Horse Fume Blanc.

CAIN CELLARS
CAIN FIVE

Moroccan Squab Pie

For a "7 x11" baking pan. Serves 12 as a first
course, 6 as a main course

6 squabs
4 yellow onions, sliced
4 cloves garlic
1 T. cinnamon
1 T nutmeg
2 cubes chicken boullion
1 T. sugar
salt & black pepper to taste
1 /4 t. saffron in 1 cup hot water
Olive oil
1/2 C. almonds, toasted slivered
1 egg yolk
2 sheets of puff pastry

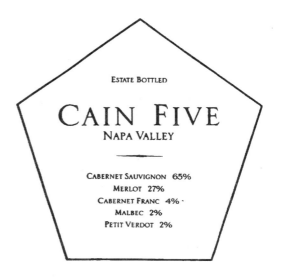

ESTATE BOTTLED

CAIN FIVE
NAPA VALLEY

CABERNET SAUVIGNON 65%
MERLOT 27%
CABERNET FRANC 4% ·
MALBEC 2%
PETIT VERDOT 2%

Saute onions in olive oil until golden brown. Add sugar and spices, and stir over moderate
heat for 2 minutes. Add squabs and remaining ingredients (except almonds) in a 4 quart pot.
Add water to completely cover the birds. Simmer gently for about 1 hour. Remove squads
from liquid and cool. De-bone and shred the meat (do not use skin) into bite-size pieces.
Return to liquid and reduce to low heat until the sauce is thickened. Add almonds, season
with salt and pepper. Place bottom layer of puff pastry into 8 buttered baking pan, fill with
meat mixture and cover with another layer of pastry. Brush top of pastry with egg yolk.
Bake at 375° until golden brown, approximately 30 minutes. Serve with a glass of Cain Five.

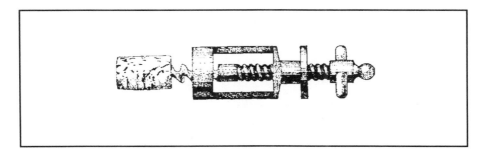

CAKEBREAD CELLARS CHARDONNAY

Cheese Puffs with Wild Mushrooms & Leeks
Makes about 3 dozen

Puff Dough:
4 oz. sweet butter, diced
1 t. salt
1 C. water
1 C. all purpose flour
4 large eggs
1/2 gruyere cheese, grated

In a heavy bottom saucepan, bring water, salt and butter to a strong boil. Stir flour in with a wooden spoon. Continue stirring until dough pulls away from the sides of the pan. Remove from heat and transfer to an electric mixer. Beat on medium speed with a paddle for 2-3 minutes to cool mixture slightly. With machine running add eggs one at a time, waiting for each egg to be incorporated before adding the next. Add cheese and place in a pastry bag with a round number 6 tip. Pipe into small mounds, about 1 to 2 inches, on sheet trays lined with parchment paper and bake in a preheated 400° oven for 20-25 minutes until golden brown. Remove to cooling racks.

Filling:
1 bunch leeks
1/2 oz. dried porcini mushrooms
1/2 lb. shiitake mushrooms, sliced

4 T. butter
3 cloves garlic, minced
salt & pepper

Cut the root and green end off the leeks. Slice the leeks in half lengthwise and chop across the grain. Cover with plenty of cold water to rinse them of any sand and dirt. Reserve.

Reconstitute the dried porcini with warm water to cover. Soak for a couple hours to soften. Remove mushrooms and chop fine. Pass liquid through a layer of cheesecloth. Reserve.

Drain leeks from water and sauté in half the butter with chopped porcini until soft and leeks have given up most of their liquid. Remove from heat and transfer to a bowl. In the same pan sauté the shiitakes with the remaining butter and garlic. Add 2 Tbsp. of the mushroom liquid and cook until dry. Add to the leeks and season with salt and pepper. Cut cheese puffs in half and stuff with a spoonfill of mushroom, leek mixture. Re-heat for 10 minutes in 300° oven. Serve warm with a glass of Cakebread Cellars Chardonnay Reserve.

GROTH VINEYARDS & WINERY
CHARDONNAY

Stuffed White Mushrooms in Phyllo

A garnish of fried carrot, leek and zucchini matchsticks add a sweet crunch to Joachim Splichal's mushroom-stuffed mushrooms.

1 stick + 2 T. unsalted butter
1 small shallot, minced
1 small garlic clove, minced
1 T. heavy cream
20 large white mushrooms, stemmed
6 oz. medium white mushrooms, chopped finely
4 oz. shiitake mushrooms, stemmed and freshly chopped
1 leek, white and tender green portions, cut into 2- by 1/4 " matchsticks
1 zucchini, cut into 2- by 1/4 " matchsticks

salt and freshly ground pepper
10 sheets of phyllo dough
2 C. vegetable oil, for frying
1 carrot, cut into 2-by 1/4" matchsticks
2 t. finely chopped parsley

In a large heavy skillet, melt 1 Tbsp. butter over high heat. Add the large mushroom caps, rounded side down, and cook until browned, about 2 minutes. Add 1/2 cup of water, cover and cook until tender, about 4 minutes longer. Using a slotted spoon, remove the mushroom caps and set aside. Pour the liquid into a small saucepan and set aside. You should have about 1/2 cup of liquid.

In a large heavy skillet, melt 1 Tbsp. of butter over high heat. When hot, add the chopped white and shiitake mushrooms, shallots and garlic and cook, stirring constantly, until softened, about 3 minutes. Stir in the cream and 1 tsp. of parsley. Season to taste with salt and pepper. Spoon this mixture into the mushroom caps and set aside to cool completely.

In a small saucepan, melt 6 Tbsp. of butter over low heat and set aside. On a work surface, cut each sheet of phyllo dough into 4 rectangles of equal size. Cover all but 2 of the rectangles with a damp towel. Using a pastry brush, lightly brush the 2 rectangles with some of the melted butter and stack them to make one layer. Center a stuffed mushroom cap, stuffed side up, on the phyllo rectangles and bring up the sides to enclose the mushroom. Pinch to seal and separate the top layers of dough like flower petals. Place on a baking sheet. Repeat with the remaining stuffed mushrooms, butter and phyllo dough.

Preheat the oven to 300°. Bake the mushrooms until the pastry is golden brown and the packages are cooked through, about 45 minutes. Meanwhile, in a heavy skillet, heat the oil over moderate heat to 350°. Add the carrots matchsticks and fry until brown and crisp,

20   *Continued...*

about 2 minutes. Using a slotted spoon, transfer to paper towels to drain thoroughly. Fry the leek matchsticks until crisp, about 1 minute; transfer to paper towels. Next, fry the zucchini matchsticks until brown and crispy, about 2-3 minutes. (The vegetables can be fried up to 1 hour ahead; keep at room temperature.)

Boil the reserved mushroom cooking liquid over high heat until reduced to 3 tsp. , about 6 minutes. Remove from the heat and whisk in the remaining 2 tsp. of butter and 1 Tbsp. parsley.

Place 5 stuffed mushrooms in the center of each large plate and spoon a generous Tbsp. of the sauce around them. Sprinkle the mushrooms with the fried vegetables and serve immediately with Groth Chardonnay.

SANFORD WINERY CHARDONNAY

Pistachio Clove Butter

Created especially by Shirley Sarvis. For attractive presentation at sit down aperitif course: provide each guest with a small ramekin or butter pot filled with the pistachio butter and a butter knife; pass baguette slices; let each guest spread on bread as he wishes. For a stand-up aperitif time: present butter in one large ramekin or crook, side with baguette slices; and let guests help themselves.

1/2 C. finely chopped lightly toasted unsalted pistachios
Tiny pinch ground cloves
Salt if necessary
l/2 C. soft unsalted butter
Thin slices of crisply, tenderly crusted non-sour French baguette

Fold nuts, along with just enough clove to be barely detectable and a few grains of salt if needed, into soft butter. Spread thickly on baguette slices. Makes about 18 canapes .

Note: Toast pistachios enough to bring up full pistachio taste, but no more. Chop pistachios into about 3/16 inch pieces. Fold nuts into butter as close to serving time as possible in order to retain their crispness.

ST. CLEMENT MERLOT

St. Clement Vineyards

Grilled Oysters with Pink Butter
By Adele Johns
Serves 4-5

2-3 Shallots minced finely
3/4 C. St. Clement Merlot (Consume the rest while cooking)
1/3 C. red wine vinegar
3/4 lb. unsalted butter, room temperature
20 small oysters

Boil shallots, wine and vinegar till reduced by 1/3. Cool slightly. With a wire wisk add butter (1 Tbsp. at a time). Keep blending until sauce is thick and smooth like pudding. Can be kept warm over a double boiler (simmering water)

Grill oysters over hot barbeque coals 3-5 minutes. Remove from grill. Remove top shell. Loosen oyster, but do not discard juice. Serve topped with spoonfull of butter, and a glass of St. Clement Vineyards Merlot.

SANFORD WINERY CHARDONNAY

Lemon-Cream-Wine Capellini

Created especially by Shirley Sarvis. Serve as first course-perhaps preceding grilled veal chops with buttered fresh green beans and/or a leaf lettuce salad. Or serve as supper main course perhaps with an appetizer of thinly sliced prosciutto rippled over crisply crusted fresh Italian or French baguette slices. Then the pasta, wine and a generosity of lightly buttered steamed fresh spinach leaves. This pasta presentation should be loose and light. Do not reduce the cream mixture to any thickness.

Continued...

1-1/2 T. unsalted butter
4 t. grated fresh lemon peel
1-1/2 T. dry white table wine
2/3 C. heavy (whipping) cream
Very small pinch of ground hot red pepper (cayenne)
4 oz. premium quality dry egg (or regular) capellini, cooked al dente in a generous amount of boiling salted water with a little olive oil, and well drained.
2 t. fresh lemon juice
2 to 3 T. freshly grated Reggiano Parmesan
Salt
Freshly ground premium quality white pepper
1 T. very finely chopped fresh curly parsley

Melt butter in a medium-sized heavy frying pan over medium heat. Add lemon peel and cook and stir for about 1 minute. Add wine and cook and stir until reduced to 2 Tbsp. total liquid. Add cream and cayenne and cook until reduced to consistency of light cream. Add hot pasta and gently turn to mingle. Remove from heat. Add lemon juice, Parmesan, and salt and pepper to taste; gently turn. Life to warm serving plates. Sprinkle with parsley. Makes 4 rich first-course or 3 supper servings.

PINE RIDGE CHARDONNAY

LUSTAU·JEREZ·1896

Skewered Tortellini
Makes 20 skewers

1 lb. tortellini (a spinach and plain mixture is visually appealing)
salt, for water
olive oil, to toss cooked pasta
6-inch bamboo skewers

Bring a large pot of lightly salted water to a boil and cook the tortellini until just tender. Drain the pasta and sprinkle with some olive oil to prevent sticking.

Put 3 warm tortellini on small, 6-inch bamboo skewers and serve immediately with Parmesan-Lemon Dip*.

Continued...

23

Parmesan Lemon Dip:
(Makes 1 cup)
1 C. creme fraiche*
1/4 C. Parmesan cheese, grated
zest of 2 lemons (zest is finely grated skin of citrus only, no white part)
juice of 2 lemons
3 cloves roasted garlic, peeled and roasted**

Combine all the ingredients for the dip in a small mixing bowl. Set aside until ready to use. Do not combine ingredients together more than 4 hours in advance.

*Creme Fraiche:
Creme fraiche is delicious served with fresh fruit and as a base for many sauces.
(Makes 4 cups)
2 C. heavy cream
2 C. buttermilk OR sour cream

Heat cream over low heat to 100°. Add buttermilk and mix well. Put in covered jar and let sit at room temperature for 6 to 8 hours. Refrigerate at least 24 hours before serving. The cream will become thick like sour cream. Creme fraiche can be kept refrigerated in a tightly covered jar for 2 to 3 weeks.

**Roasted Garlic:
Roasted garlic tends to be sweeter and milder than raw or sautéed garlic and is even delicious as a vegetable.

several heads of garlic, cut in half across the middle
olive oil

Preheat oven to 350°. Toss cut garlic heads lightly in olive oil. Bake for 1 hour, or until golden brown and soft. Preserve individual garlic cloves in olive oil for 2 to 3 weeks.

Wine is ♥ smart
Enjoy in moderation

PINE RIDGE
CHENIN BLANC

**PINE RIDGE
WINERY**

Phyllo Spring Rolls

The best feature of this recipe is that the spring rolls are baked, not fried, and the filling can incorporate any leftovers for an easy hors d'oeuvres. All ingredients are available nationally in supermarkets in the Asian food section

Filling:

4 T. peanut oil OR olive oil
3 green onion, cut into 2" long thin strips
2 carrots, cut into 2" long thin strips
1/2 yellow onion, cut into small squares
2 T. fresh ginger, grated OR 1 T. powdered ginger

2 C. fresh bean sprouts
1 T. garlic, minced
1/2 C. assorted mushrooms, chopped
1/2 C. canned water chestnuts, chopped

Add oil to skillet and heat. Add above ingredients and cook until tender. Add the following seasonings:

1/4 t. sesame oil
1 T. soy sauce
1 T. rice wine vinegar

salt to taste
pepper to taste

Toss ingredients and seasoning well. When cooled slightly, add following to above mixture and drain excess oil:
1-1/2 C. mixed greens
2" long strips - use fresh spinach or mixed greens lettuce mix

To make spring rolls:
1 lb. phyllo dough, thawed (paper thin pastry found in freezer section)
1/2 C. melted butter OR margarine
pastry brush OR paper towel

Lay out 1 sheet phyllo dough. Cut into 3 pieces: one 8" wide strip and two 4" wide strips. Lay 8" wide sheet down first, brush lightly with melted butter, then lay down the two 4" wide strips on top of each other in the center of the 8" piece. Place a small amount of cooled filling, approximately 1/4 cup at the bottom center of phyllo. Lightly brush exposed pastry with melted butter. Roll loosely, bottom to top, folding side edges of dough over halfway to seal ends. Brush completed spring roll with melted butter. Repeat procedure until all filling is used. Refrigerate until ready to use covered in plastic wrap (can be made 2 days in advance) or kept frozen up to 3 months. For serving: bake spring rolls on cookie sheet until golden brown at 375° oven, about 10 minutes. Serve with Chinese yellow mustard as a dipping sauce.

25

SEGHESIO WINERY
CABERNET SAUVIGNON

Italian Sausage Stuffed Mushrooms
Serves 4-6

18 - 20 large mushrooms
1/2 lb. Italian sausage (hot or mild)
1/2 C. chopped onion
3 - 6 cloves fresh garlic, minced
1/4 C. freshly grated Parmesan cheese

3 - 4 T. olive oil
1/4 - 1/3 C. Seghesio Cabernet Sauvignon
1/4 C. Italian seasoned bread crumbs
1 egg

Preheat oven to 350°. Remove stems from mushrooms. Chop stems. Brown the sausage, onion, garlic and chopped stems in olive oil. Drain well. Add wine to drained mixture and simmer until liquid is slightly reduced. Remove from heat. Mix in bread crumbs, egg & cheese. Stuff mushroom slightly over full. Bake at 350° for 15 - 20 minutes. Sprinkle with extra Parmesan cheese before serving. Serve with a glass of Seghesio Cabernet Sauvignon.

FROG'S LEAP
SAUVIGNON BLANC

Prawn Bar-b-que

We love getting a whole group of people together for an informal Bar-B-Que at Frog's Leap. The first course needs to be quick, festive, tasty, and go very well with our Sauvignon Blanc.

Medium to large-sized fresh prawns, 4 or more per person (unshelled)
Fresh garlic
Dill, basil or other favorite garden herb
Red Pepper flakes
Virgin olive oil
1 bottle Frog's Leap Sauvignon Blanc
Salt & pepper to taste

30-60 minutes ahead of serving, lightly rinse the prawns, drain and place in a shallow glass bowl. Toss with about 1/4 cup oil, add crushed garlic, pepper flakes   *Continued...*

(don't be shy!) and minced herbs to taste. Add a pinch of sea salt and pepper. Seal with saran wrap. 10 minutes prior to serving, toss with about 1/4 cup of Sauvignon Blanc.

(**Note:** *a crisp, fruity Sauvignon Blanc complements the shellfish, with a touch of herbs and just a hint of spice. Sauvignon Blanc can be very compatible with garlic!*)

To grill, pour yourself a glass of chilled wine and start the fire. Place the prawns on the grill, turn quickly as the shells change to a bright pink color. Serve in a warm, shallow bowl garnished with sprigs of the herbs. Accompany with fresh, savory bread and wine. Keep the napkins handy!

CAKEBREAD CELLARS CHARDONNAY

Smoked Trout, Watercress, Pears and Fresh Dill on Belgian Endive Spears
Serves 8

2 smoked trout (1/3 lb. each)
1/2 C. watercress (pick leaves off of stems)
1/2 pear
2 Belgian endive

Vinaigreffe:
1/2 lemon
1 t. Dijon mustard
1/2 C. vegetable oil   1 t. fresh dill, chopped
freshly ground white pepper   salt

Remove head, tail and skin from trout. Break into small pieces and discard any loose bones. Toss with watercress leaves. Peel and core pear. Chop into a fine dice and add to smoked trout. Reserve.

Whisk lemon juice and mustard together. Slowly drizzle in oil to emulsify. Add chopped dill and season with ground white pepper and salt. Toss smoked trout mixture with vinaigrette to lightly coat.

Peel the larger leaves off the outside of the Belgian Endive and fill with a spoonful of smoked trout mixture. Serve cold with a glass of Cakebread Cellars Chardonnay.

SOUPS

OAK RIDGE VINEYARDS
FUME BLANC

Bean Soup

2 1/2 C. bean mix
4 ham hocks
1 lg. onion, chopped
2-3 cloves garlic, chopped
16 oz. can chopped tomatoes

16 oz. can tomatoes and green chilies
2 C. Oak Ridge Vineyards Fume Blanc
2 qts. fresh water
juice of 1 lemon
salt & pepper

Rinse beans well. Cover with water and soak 6 hours to overnight. Drain. Put beans in 6 quarts water and Fume Blanc: add onion ham hocks, garlic, tomatoes and lemon juice. Bring to a boil, stir, then simmer for about 4 hours. Add salt and pepper to taste. May be refrigerated covered. The flavor improves overnight, so it's best made the day before you serve it.

HUSCH VINEYARDS
PINOT NOIR

Portuguese Soup

6 C. water
1 lb. potatoes, peeled and cut into chunks
2-3 garlic cloves
1 medium onion, chopped
1 carrot, chopped
1 small green pepper, chopped
3 T. olive oil
1/2 t. basil
1 C. Husch Pinot Noir
1 bunch kale or Swiss chard washed and chopped

2 ham hocks
1-1/2 lb. beans
1 bay leaf
1-15 oz. can tomatoes (or 3 larger whole)
1 stalk celery
2-3 cloves garlic, crushed
1 t. oregano
salt and pepper

Combine beans and six cups water, soak overnight. The next day pour into soup pot without draining. Add ham hocks, whole garlic and 1 bay leaf. Cook 2-3 hours until ham hocks are done, adding potatoes after one hour. Remove ham hocks and cut meat off bone when done.

Sauté cut up vegetables in olive oil with garlic, oregano, basil, salt and pepper. Combine vegetables, ham hoch meat, kale, tomatoes and Husch wine into bean pot and cook for 1 hour or longer. Can be put in refrigerator and reheated the next day. Serve with fresh bread and Husch Pinot Noir.

GROTH VINEYARDS & WINERY
SAUVIGNON BLANC

Groth

Corn Chowder with Cumin and Red Pepper

Groth Sauvignon Blanc, because of the lively, grapefruity flavors, and the tropical herbaceous characteristics pairs very well with vegetable flavors and seafood.

2 T. butter
1 onion, chopped
1/4 C. Groth Sauvignon Blanc
1 T. cumin seed roasted and ground
2 C. chicken stock

2 1/2 C. fresh corn
1 T. oregano
2 C. milk
salt and pepper to taste
1 red bell pepper, diced

Sauté onion with cumin. Add the wine and de-glaze the pan and reduce. Add stock and bring to a boil. Add corn and oregano and simmer for 15 minutes. Puree with milk, add salt and pepper. Reheat adding diced red pepper. (sautéd clams or shrimp make a nice surprise.)

SUTTER HOME
CHARDONNAY

SUTTER HOME

Fish Market Cioppino with Chardonnay

2 T. olive oil
1 large onion, sliced thinly
2 cloves garlic, presses or minced
1/4 C. chopped Italian Parsley
1/2 t. each dried oregano and thyme
1/3 lb. each bay scallops and cooked shrimp
1 can (14 - 1/2 oz.) reduced salt chicken broth

1 can (14-1/2 oz.) clam juice
1 C. Sutter Home Chardonnay
2 T. catsup or chili sauce
1 bay leaf
1 lb. clams (optional)
salt and ground black pepper

1 bunch leeks, ends trimmed, cut in half lengthwise, rinsed, and diagonally sliced 1/2" thick
2/3 lb. firm white fish fillets (snapper or rock cod), de-boned and cut into 1-1/2" chunks.

In a 5-6 quart pan, combine oil, onion, leeks, garlic, parsley, oregano, and thyme. Cook over medium-high, stirring occasionally until onion is limp, about 5 minutes. Add tomatoes with juice, clam juice, chardonnay wine, chicken broth, catsup, and bay leaf. Bring to a boil over high heat: cover and simmer until flavors are blended, about 15 minutes. Add fish chunks, scallops and clams, cover and simmer until clams open, about 5 minutes. Discard unopened clams. Stir in shrimp and simmer about 1 minute more, until shrimp are hot. Season to taste. Accompany with crusty bread, long celery and carrot sticks, and Sutter Home Chardonnay.

EBERLE WINERY
CHARDONNAY

Corn & Crayfish Soup

3/4 C. bacon, cut in 1/2 inch pieces
1 C. chopped leek, white part only
1/4 C. chopped shallot
1 T. chopped serrano chili
1 C. Eberle Chardonnay   1 T. minced garlic
16 C. fresh corn kernels   3 qt. chicken stock
8 ounces cooked crayfish- tail meat   1 to 1-1/2 C. heavy cream
4 C. chanterelle mushrooms, trimmed, not larger than 1/2-inch across

In a large soup pot, render fat from bacon, then remove bacon and reserve leaving the fat in the pot. Cook the leek, shallot, chili and garlic in the bacon fat till tender, but not browned.

Add corn and white wine and cook till the liquid is gone, then add chicken stock and simmer for 20 minutes. Puree soup in a blender, then strain and return the soup to the pot.

Meanwhile, in a frying pan, cook chanterelles in a little butter till done, then add the crayfish and cook gently about one minute more, season with a little salt and fresh ground black pepper and a Tbsp. of thyme. Add mushrooms and crayfish to the soup and bring it to a simmer; add cream, season to taste with salt and pepper, simmer one minute more, then serve. Garnish each bowl with a few pieces of th reserved bacon and some chives.

Walford uses applewood smoked bacon which gives the soup a distinctive character, but you can substitute another bacon. You can also substitute another mushroom for the chanterelles and shrimp for the crayfish, but it really won't be the same soup.

31

IRON HORSE VINEYARDS
WEDDING CUVEE CHAMPAGNE

Cream of Green Lentil Soup

1 lb. green lentils	1 T. tomato paste
2 T. olive oil	2 qts. water
1/2 lb. pancetta cut into small cubes	1 C. heavy cream
12 shallots peeled	Salt and pepper to taste

Rinse lentils thoroughly. Heat olive oil in large heavy soup pot over medium heat; add half the pancetta and onions and cook for 10 minutes until brown. Add the water, lentils and tomato paste; bring to a boil and cook for 40 minutes or until lentils are soft.

Slowly add the cream, so as not to curdle; season with salt and pepper and cook for ten minutes. Pour the soup into a blender or food processor and puree to a smooth texture. Saute the rest of the pancetta until crisp; chop coarsely.

Heat soup, pour into bowls and sprinkle with pancetta.

Wine Notes:
We chose our Iron Horse 1990 Wedding Cuvee to go with this dish as the sparkling will cut through the righness of the soup. The Wedding Cuvee is our Blanc de Noirs made from 100 percent Pinot Noir. It has a slight salmon hue and is naturally rich and round. This is the most romantic of our Sparklings and dangerously easy to drink.

SEGHESIO WINERY SANGIOVESE

Minestone

"Minestrone is an old world recipe and I know there are different ways to make it. The one I use was given to me by my husband's mother, Angela Seghesio who with her husband, Eduardo founded Seghesio Winery. Minestrone is tasty in any season but Angela, especially enjoyed making it, when her vegetable garden was at its peak in early summer. One of her favorite vegetables that she put in her homemade soup was Italian beans."

Soak one pound of red kidney beans in 6 or 8 cups of cold water overnight or for several hours in the morning. Simmer them until tender.

Chop 6 oz. of salt pork with 4 cloves garlic, 1 medium onion, 1/2 cup parsley, 4 leaves basil and 1 stalk celery. Brown these ingredients in 2 tablespoons oil and 2 tablespoons butter along with 3 whole tomatoes, skinned, cut and squeezed. Use garden fresh, if available or else canned. When these ingredients have cooked together for 30 - 45 minutes, strain them into a kettle containing 20-25 cups of boiling water.

Pour the water, in which you have simmered the beans, into the same boiling kettle. Mash 1/2 of the beans and add them also. To this pour 8 oz canned tomato sauce.

Then add these vegetables in the following order:
remainder of red kidney beans
1-1/2 cups green beans, cut into 1 inch lengths
1 stalk celery, sliced
1 carrot, cut in half and sliced
1 potato, peeled and cubed

After these cook for 15 minutes, add:
2 small zucchini, cut in half and sliced
3-5 leaves if Swiss chard
1 leek, sliced, use mostly the white part
1/4 lb. spaghetti or elbow macaroni, uncooked

Salt and pepper to taste. Simmer for another 20 minutes. Serve the parmesan cheese and French bread. Will serve 10-12 people.

SEBASTIANI VINEYARDS
CHARDONNAY

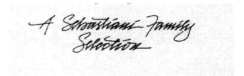

Quick Minestrone
Serves 6

1-11oz. can red kidney beans	1 t. salt
1/2 t. garlic salt	1 clove garlic, pressed
1/4 t. pepper	1 T. oil
1/4 C. chopped parsley	2 stalks celery, chopped
1 small carrot, diced	2 green onions, chopped
4 to 5 leaves Swiss chard, chopped	3 T. butter
8-ounce can tomato sauce	2-1/2 C. water
1/2 C. Sebastiani Chardonnay	Grated Parmesan cheese

1/4 C. uncooked elbow macaroni (optional)
1 small zucchini, not peeled, cut into small cubes

Place undrained beans in a large kettle or saucepan; mash about two-thirds of the beans and leave the rest whole. Add salt, garlic salt, garlic, pepper, oil, and parsley, stirring well. Then add all the vegetables, butter, tomato sauce, and water. Simmer 1 hour or more and then add wine. (If desired macaroni may be added at this point.) Simmer 10 to 15 minutes longer. Sprinkle with cheese before serving. If soup seems too thick, add more water and salt to taste. Serve with Sebastiani Sonoma Chardonnay.

CAIN CELLARS
CAIN FIVE

Chestnut Soup
Serves 6

4 C. veal stock
1 - 10 oz. can of chestnut puree
1/4 C. port wine
1 cube chicken bouillon
1 C. half & half
1/2 lb. shallots, chopped and sautéed

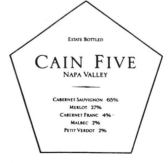

tarragon to taste
black pepper to taste

Pour stock, shallots and chestnut puree into a food processor or blender, puree. Transfer into a cooking pot with remaining ingredients. Simmer gently for 15 minutes. Serve hot. Serve with a glass of Cain Five.

SANFORD WINERY
PINOT NOIR-VIN GRIS

Herb Vegetable Beef Soup

3/4 lb. lean ground beef round
1/3 C. Sanford Vin Gris-Pinot Noir
1/2 t. crumbled dry thyme
1-1/2 celery, sliced diagonally

1 C. onions, finely chopped
1/2 t. fresh rosemary, finely chopped
3 C. mild lean beef broth
salt

1-1/2 C. carrots, peeled diagonally, sliced 3/16" thick
1 large can (1 lb., 12 oz.) peeled whole tomatoes, broken up

In a large heavy kettle over medium heat, cook beef until crumbly and lightly browned. Add onions and cook until limp. Add wine and cook until it disappears. Add rosemary, thyme, tomatoes, broth, carrots, celery and about 1/4 tsp. salt. Cover and simmer slowly for 1-1/2 to 3 hours. Correct seasoning with salt. Garnish each serving with a fresh sprig of rosemary. Makes 4 main-course servings. Serve soup, wine, crusty non-sour French rolls, and cold fresh pears for dessert and you have a super supper.

RODNEY STRONG VINEYARDS
SAUVIGNON BLANC

Chilled Curried Zucchini Soup
Recipe courtesy of Charlotte Strong

2 lbs. Zucchini
1 t. Curry
2 C. Canned chicken broth

1 C. scallions, minced
1 t. Cumin, ground
3 C. Buttermilk

In a large saucepan sweat (sauté very slowly, as not to brown) 2 pounds of zucchini (scrubbed, trimmed and chopped) and 1 cup minced scallions in 6 tablespoons of butter over moderate heat for 15 minutes or until zucchini is soft. Add 1 tablespoon of curry and 1 table-spoon of ground cumin, cook stirring for 2 minutes. Stir in 2 cups of canned chicken broth. In a food processor, puree the mixture in small batches. Transfer puree to large bowl, stir in 3 cups of buttermilk. Salt and pepper to taste. Chill for at least 4 hours. Soup may be thinned with broth or buttermilk. Serves 6.

(This is quite spicy. Use 2 teaspoons curry and 2 teaspoons cumin for milder flavor.)

GROTH VINEYARDS & WINERY
SAUVIGNON BLANC

Zucchini Soup

3-4 lbs. zucchini cut into chunks
1 lb. bacon, crisped and crumbled
2-1/2 C. chicken stock
1/2 C. Groth Sauvignon Blanc
1 onion, chopped
3 cloves garlic, crushed
1 bay leaf
4 dashes tobasco
salt and pepper to taste

Put ingredients into a large pot
and bring to a boil. Simmer for 30
minutes. Let cool, remove bay
leaf and then process in a blender.
Re-heat to serve. Serves 8.

SALADS

CLOS PEGASE
CHARDONNAY

Cheese Mousse

CLOS PEGASE

4 oz. cottage cheese
1 lemon
1/2 pint cold water
2 T. chopped chives or spring onion

4 oz. cream cheese
1 T. powdered gelatin
egg white

Blend smoothly two cheeses. Add the finely grated lemon rind and blend well. Soften the gelatin in 2-3 tablespoons cold water; when the gelatin has dissolved, add to the rest of the water and make sure it is mixed. Spoon this into the cheese and lemon rind, beat well; allow to cool but not set. When the cheese mixture begins to stiffen slightly, fold in the stiffly beaten egg whites. Rinse out a mold or brush lightly with oil and refrigerate it to set.

SUTTER HOME
CHENIN BLANC

SUTTER HOME

Chicken Salad with Chenin Blanc

1-1/2 lbs chicken breast halves, skinned
1 whole green onion
1 quarter-size slice fresh ginger (optional), crushed

1/2 C. Sutter Home Chenin Blanc
1-1/2 C. water

Dressing:
3 T. vegetable oil
2 T. Sutter Home Chenin Blanc
1/4 t. crushed red pepper
1 t. each green onion, minced, and cilantro
2 t. each white wine vinegar and oriental sesame oil

2 T. creamy peanut butter
2 T. each sugar & low sodium soy sauce
cilantro sprigs
2 qts. (3/4 to 1 lb.) shredded lettuce

Place chicken breasts in a 2-quart pan. Add wine, whole green onion, ginger, and water. Bring to a boil, cover and simmer for 20 minutes. Remove from heat and let stand until chicken is cool enough to handle. Strain broth and reserve. Remove chicken from bones, then pull meat into long shreds.

Dressing: In a bowl, blend together vegetable oil and peanut butter. Add Wine, sugar, soy sauce, vinegar, sesame oil, crushed red pepper, green onion, and cilantro. Mound lettuce on individual plates. Arrange shredded chicken over lettuce. Drizzle dressing over all. Makes 4 servings. Serve with Sutter Home Chenin Blanc.

PINE RIDGE CHARDONNAY

Tarragon-Orange Vinaigrette
Makes 1-3/4 cups

2/3 C. orange juice
salt, to taste
2 T. shallots, finely minced
1/2 C. fresh tarragon, chopped OR 2 T. dried tarragon

2 T. Dijon-style mustard
pepper to taste
1 C. best-quality olive oil

Combine orange juice, mustard, salt, and pepper. Stir until salt is dissolved. Add tarragon and shallots. Whisk in olive oil until well blended.

QUIVIRA VINEYARDS CHARDONNAY

Avocado and Melon Salad

Assorted melons: Honeydew, Persian or Cantalope
2-3 ripe avocados
1/4 C. raspberry vinegar
1/2 t. Dijon mustard
several grinds of pepper

1/2 t. salt
1/2 C. walnut oil
1 T chopped fresh tarragon

Avocados and melons maybe sliced and laid fan shaped on lettuce leaves, then dressed with above dressing or the fruit maybe cubed, tossed with dressing and served on a bed of lettuce. Another delicious combination using this dressing is honeydew melon and tomatoes treated in the same fashion.

39

FICKLIN VINEYARDS
TINTA PORT

Cranberry Port Melange
Serves 4-6

Two whole oranges, one for salad, one for garnish
3/4 cup Ficklin Tinta Port
1 package (3 ounces) raspberry-flavored gelatin
1 can (16 ounces) whole cranberry sauce
1/2 C. chopped walnuts or pecans
Orange slices and parsley for garnish
Sour cream (optional)

Chop one orange in grinder or blender. Place the ground orange and the Tinta Port into a small saucepan and bring to a boil. Allow to boil briskly for about 1 minute. Add the raspberry-flavored gelatin and stir until dissolved. Add the cranberry sauce and nuts. Mix together. Place in a mold and chill. To unmold salad, briefly place mold in a bowl of warm water. Invert onto plate, garnish with sliced orange slices and parsley. Try serving with a dollop of sour cream on top.

IRON HORSE VINEYARDS
PINOT NOIR

Pear & Pomegranate Salad

3 C. argugula
3 pomegranates
9 pricely pears
2 T. walnut oil
Salt and pepper

Place greens in a large bowl. Remove seeds from two pomegranates and set aside. Juice one pomegranate. Cut pricely pears in half lengthwise and scoop out fruit. Toss greens with juice of one pomegranate, walnut oil and salt and pepper.

Place greens on six chilled plates, scatter pomegranate seeds over salads and three pieces of pear. Serve with sheeps milk, ricotta, or another young soft cheese.

ST CLEMENT
SAUVIGNON BLANC

Fiesta Winter Salad
Serves 6

1 large head Romaine lettuce torn into bite size pieces
1 medium size red onion thinly sliced into rings
1 - 8 oz can of mandarin oranges, drained
1 large avocado sliced into bite size pieces

Combine all but the avocado in large salad bowl. Chill until ready to serve and add avocado and dressing.

Dressing:
1 T. Dijon type mustard
1 T. wine vinegar
1/2 C. olive oil
1 t. tarragon leaves, OR T toasted sesame seeds

Combine all the above. Salt and pepper to taste. Serve with St. Clement Sauvignon Blanc

SANFORD WINERY
PINOT NOIR-VIN GRIS

Coriander Duck Salad

4 oz. lean skinless meat of roasted or simmered duck (Long Island or Petaluma), torn into julienne slivers
1 C. fresh coriander leaves (tender leaves only, no stems), and additional coriander sprigs for garnish
Salt and freshly ground black pepper
2-1/2 to 3 T. clean and light olive oil or other salad oil
12 cuplets of the small leaves of very fresh and crisp iceberg lettuce, each about 2-1/2 inches in diameter

Turn duck, coriander leaves, and salt and pepper to season generously with enough oil to cloak. Loosely and generously pile salad into lettuce cups. Arrange on platter. Garnish generously with coriander sprigs. Makes about 12 appetizers.

BUENA VISTA WINERY
CHARDONNAY

Oriental Smoked Game Hen Salad
Serves 4

1 Cornish game hen, meat cut into 1" pieces
3 - 4 green onions, thinly sliced lengthwise 1"
2 carrots, peeled, sliced into 1" julienne
1 cucumber, peeled, seeded, sliced into 1" julienne
4-5 romaine lettuce leaves, sliced into 1" strips
4 oz. rice noodles, boiled until soft, cut into 4" pieces
2 t. sesame seeds
Oriental dressing (recipe follows)

Place all ingredients in a large bowl. Toss and pour on oriental dressing; toss again.
Sprinkle with sesame seeds and serve.

Oriental Dressing:
1/3 C. soy sauce
2 T. hoisio sauce
1/4 C. rice vinegar
2 quarter-size slices fresh ginger, minced
2 cloves fresh garlic, peeled and minced

1 t. sesame oil
1/4 C. peanut oil

Whisk all ingredients together, except oils. Slowly add oils whisking constantly.

RODNEY STRONG VINEYARDS CHARDONNAY

RODNEY STRONG

Orzo & Artichoke Salad
Recipe courtesy of Charlotte Strong, serves 4

1-1/2 C. Orzo (rice-shaped pasta)
9 oz. pkg Frozen artichoke hearts, thawed
1 Large egg yolk
1 t. Dijon mustard
2 T. Fresh basil, minced
2 T. Fresh lemon juice
4 Scallions, minced

3/4 C. Olive oil
1/2 C. Canned chicken broth
2 T. White wine vinegar
2 oz. Prosciutto or pancetta, minced
2 oz. Fresh grated parmesan cheese
1/4 C. Parsley, minced

Cook orzo in salted water 7-8 minutes. Drain and rinse under cold water. Toss in 1/4 cup of the olive oil. Simmer artichoke hearts in chicken broth for 6-7 minutes or until tender. Drain and add to orzo. In a small bowl, whisk together the egg yolk, vinegar, mustard, salt and pepper (to taste). Add 1/2 cup olive oil in a stream whisking and add basil. Pour over orzo. Add prosciutto, parmesan, lemon juice, parsley, and scallions. Toss and enjoy.

FETZER VINEYARDS CHARDONNAY

Sundial Pasta Salad with Corn & Chilies

1/2 lb. small pasta shells
2 T. light olive oil

Dressing:

3/4 t. hot red chili flakes
1/4 C. white wine vinegar
3 T. light corn syrup
2 bay leaves

1 t. fresh jalapeno chile, minced (optional)
1/4 C. Fetzer Sundial Chardonnay
2 T. lime or lemon juice

2 C. fresh sweet corn kernels
1/4 C. green onions, minced
1/4 C. fresh basil or parsley, chopped

1/2 C. red bell pepper, finely diced
1/4 black olives, pitted and slivered
salt and freshly ground pepper to taste

Cook pasta in 6 quarts of lightly salted water until just done (al dente). Drain, cool, and toss with olive oil. Set aside in a bowl.

In a small sauce pan, add the dressing ingredients, bring to a boil and simmer for 3 minutes. Add optional fresh chile if you want an zestier flavor. Remove bay leaves and cool dressing. Add corn, bell pepper, onions, olives and basil to bowl with pasta. Pour the cooled dressing over and toss gently. Serves 4. Enjoy with a glass of Fetzer Sundial Chardonnay.

CLOS PEGASE CHARDONNAY

CLOS PEGASE

Shrimp and Crab Mold

3 T. cold water
1 can cream of mushroom soup
1 C. mayonnaise
1 can crab
1 C. celery, chopped

1 pkg. gelatin
6 oz. cream cheese
12 oz. boiled shrimp
2 green onions, chopped

Dissolve gelatin in water. Heat soup and add gelatin, cream cheese, and mayonnaise. Blend well. Add other ingredients and put in a mold.

SANFORD WINERY
PINOT NOIR-VIN GRIS

Spinach-Capellini Salad

Created especially by Shirley Sarvis. Adjust pasta seasoning to make a salad which is fully tasty, yet with the pasta mellowness present. Serve salad at room temperature.

2 qts. fresh tender washed spinach leaves, stems removed (loosely pack to measure)
2 ozs. premium quality capellini (dry pasta without egg, cooked al dente in boiling salted water with a little olive oil, and well drained)
Light, fresh olive oil (such as Sasso in the green can)
4 t. finest snippings of sun-dried tomatoes (drained from their oil)
1/4 oz very fresh finely ground premium quality white pepper
1-1/2 t. fresh lemon juice
1/2 oz very finely fresh grated well-aged dry Jack cheese (cheese should have 12 to 15 months of age)
Salt
24 tender uncooked spinach leaves, each about 3-1/2 by 2-1/2 inches, washed and dried

Cook spinach until tender; drain well, and squeeze out excess moisture (you should have about 1/2 cup). Cut into small shreds about 1/2 or 1/4 inch. Toss hot just-cooked capellini with about 1/4 cup oil. Gently mix in about 6 Tbsp. of the cooked spinach, the tomatoes, lemon juice, pepper, 2 Tbsp. (about one-half) of the Jack cheese and salt to season well.

 Just before serving, arrange whole spinach leaves on a serving platter; brush each with olive oil to lightly cloak. With a fork, make coils of the salad 1-1/2 inches in diameter (include a nice proportion of all salad ingredients in each coil) and place one in center of each leaf. Add a little more oil to each coil for gloss. Sprinkle very lightly with a little of the remaining cheese. Guests lift an individual salad with fingers. Makes at least 24 appetizers.

CLOS PEGASE
CHARDONNAY

Chilled Tofu Timbale with Chives
Serves 4

4 T. lemon juice
1 lb. cold soft tofu, drained and rinsed
Coarse salt

2 T. olive oil
2 T. chopped chives
Chive spears (optional)

On 4 rimmed salad plates, spoon equal amounts of lemon juice and oil; swirl together and sprinkle liberally with salt. Cut tofu into 8 equal pieces; set two on each plate. Garnish with chives.

PINE RIDGE
MERLOT

Grilled Vegetable and Frisee Salad
Serves 4-6

1/2 C. olive oil
1 t. pepper
1 clove garlic, crushed
1/2 C. olive oil
1/2 t. pepper
1/4 balsamic vinegar
1 green zucchini, sliced 1/4" thick sticks, lengthwise
1 leek, white part only, cut into 4 pieces lengthwise
8 large asparagus stalks, trimmed
2 each shallots, peeled and sliced thinly

1 t. salt
1 T. fresh rosemary, chopped
1 red bell pepper, quartered & seeded
1/2 t. salt
1 T. Dijon mustard

5 cups mixed lettuces that are sturdy, as warm dressing will wilt delicate lettuces: frisee, watercress, escarole, endive. Mix olive oil, salt, pepper, rosemary, and garlic together. Toss vegetables in herbed oil. Grill vegetables until just cooked. Brush with olive oil as needed to prevent sticking. Cut into bite size pieces when cool. Sauté shallots in olive oil until soft. Stir in salt and pepper and let dissolve. Add Dijon mustard and vinegar and whisk over low heat until incorporated. Pour over mixed greens.

Serve room temperature or slightly warm vegetables arranged over bed of lettuce.

SIDE DISH

CUVAISON
PINOT NOIR

Tete de Moine Biscuits
By Chef Jeffrey Young

2 C. all-purpose flour
1 T. double-acting baking powder
1/2 t. salt
1 - 1/2 C. coarsely grated Tete de Moine cheese
2 T. chopped rosemary
3 - 3/4 C. heavy cream

Preheat oven to 425°. Into a bowl, sift together the flour, baking powder and salt. Add Tete de Moine cheese and rosemary. Combine well. Add cream and mix until it forms a dough. Gather the dough into a ball, knead it gently 6 times on a lightly floured surface. Roll or pat it out to 1/2 inch thick. Dip 2 - 1/2 inch round cutter in flour and cut dough into rounds. Gather the scraps, re-roll the dough, and cut our more rounds in the same manner.

Transfer the rounds to an ungreased baking sheet. Bake in the middle of preheated oven for 15 to 17 minutes, or until they are golden. Transfer to a wire rack and allow to cool for 5 minutes. Makes about 12 biscuits.

SHAFER VINEYARDS
CABERNET SAUVIGNON

Gratin of Potato and Wild Rice

4 Potatoes, peeled and thinly sliced
1 Pint Cream
White pepper, freshly ground to taste

1 C. Wild rice, cooked
Salt to taste
2 T. Butter

Butter a baking dish (approximately 6" x 10"). Place one layer of potatoes, alternating lightly with wild rice until full. Scald cream with salt and pepper. Pour over potatoes. Cover with foil and place into a 350° oven for approximately 45 minutes. Allow to set five to ten minutes before serving. Serve with *Encrusted Rack of Lamb* (see index).

PINE RIDGE CHARDONNAY

Lacy Potato Pancakes
Serves 6

2 large eggs, beaten
1/2 t. salt
1/4 C. green onions, chopped, white part only
2 baking potatoes, peeled and kept in cold water until ready to use
vegetable oil for frying

1/2 C. flour
1/4 C. beer

In large bowl, mix together the eggs, flour, salt, beer, and green onions. Set aside.

Grate the potatoes with large hole grater. Squeeze out any moisture and add the potatoes to the batter. Blend well and, using wet hands, form 2-1/2-inch loosely packed pancakes. As you make them, drop them into a skillet containing 1/2-inch of hot vegetable oil. Fry for 3 to 4 minutes on each side or until golden brown. You will have to do this in batches. Drain the pancakes on paper towels and keep warm in a low temperature oven until ready to serve.

ST. SUPERY SAUVIGNON BLANC

Lemon Risotto

2 T. olive oil
1 small onion, chopper finely
6 C. chicken broth
zest of 1 lemon

1 clove garlic, minced
1-1/2 C. arborio rice
juice of 1 lemon
1/3 C. grated parmesan cheese

In a large pot sauté garlic in olive oil until lightly browned. Add onion and sauté until translucent. Pour in rice and stir five or six times until all the rice is coated. Over medium heat and maintaining a boil, add broth slowly to the rice, ladle by ladle, stirring the rice until each ladel of broth is absorbed before adding the next ladel. (This is a slow process and takes about 20 minutes of stirring. The rice creates its own creamy sauce, yet remains firm and delicious.) The rice is done when the kernels of rice are soft all the way through. (Underdone risotto has a slightly chalky quality when the kernel is bitten into.) Add lemon juice, lemon zest and cheese, stir, cover and let stand for two minutes before serving. Serves six.

SEGHESIO WINERY CHARDONNAY

Risotto

"Angela Seghesio, the wife of Eduardo Seghesio - the two founders of Seghesio Winery - would often prepare risotto for wine buyers who traveled by train from San Francisco to Chianti in the early 1900's. They built the Victorian home which appears on the Seghesio label. Today their son, Eugene Pete Seghesio and his wife Rachel Ann live in the home. Angela raised her own chickens and would use one in making risotto. Chickens, when old, have lots of flavor. Living in the original Seghesio family home - I am now known as "Mama Seghesio" - cooking and preparing dinner for many guests involved in the wine business from all over the United States. I often serve risotto, and our guests enjoy it." Serves 10 to 12.

Chicken Broth:
1 stewing hen
2 carrots
1 onion, quartered

3 qts water
2 stalks celery with leaves
1 leek

Rice:
2 cups dried mushrooms
1/2 C. butter
salt and pepper

1 large onion, minced
3 C. rice
1 1/2 C. grated Parmesan cheese

Chicken Broth: Place the stewing hen in stock pot of water. Simmer for 45 minutes. Add the carrots, celery, onion and leek. Simmer for 1 1/2 hours. Strain the broth and skim off fat.

Soak the mushrooms in hot water for 15 minutes and thinly slice. Sauté the onion in butter. When delicately brown, add the mushrooms and cook about 15 minutes. Add the rice and stir constantly for about 15 minutes. Add the chicken broth 1 cup at a time, cook for about 45 minutes. Add the salt and pepper. When the rice reaches the al dente (chewy) state, remove from heat and add the Parmesan cheese. Serve immediately and pass with more cheese.

Note: Chicken broth can be made the day before. If made the day before, refrigerate and skim off the fat the next day.

SEGHESIO WINERY CHARDONNAY

Risotto Milanese

2 T. olive oil
1 yellow onion, chopped
l/2 C. Seghesio Chardonnay
3-1/2 C. chicken stock
1/4 - 1/2 C. freshly grated Parmesan cheese
1 oz. dried porcini mushrooms, rehydrated in 1/4 C. water
Freshly ground pepper to taste

2 T. butter
1 C. arborio rice
1 clove garlic, minced
1/4 t. saffron

Simmer chicken stock in separate pan. Sauté onions in olive oil and butter until onions are clear. Add rice to onions, sautéing for 5 minutes. (It is important to stir constantly from the time the rice is added until the rice is tender.) Add wine and garlic to mixture and allow liquid to cook down. Then add 1/2 cup of warm stock and rehydrated mushrooms with their liquid. Allow liquid to cook down. As the liquid simmers away, continue adding 1/2 cup of warm stock. Repeat this process until the rice is tender, approximately 30 minutes. With the last 1/2 cup of stock, add the saffron. When rice is tender, stir in 1/4 - 1/2 cup of Parmesan cheese and freshly ground pepper to taste. Serve immediately.

Serves 2 as a main dish and 4 as a side dish. Serve with the Seghesio Chardonnay.

OAK RIDGE VINEYARDS CHARDONNEY

Oak Ridge Vineyards

Savory Rice Pilaf

1 - 10 oz. can onion soup
1 C. regular rice, uncooked
1 C. fresh mushrooms, sliced
1/4 C. Oak Ridge Vineyards Chardonnay

1/2 C. water
1/4 C. butter

Combine soup, wine and water; heat. Sauté rice in butter until transparent and yellow. Add mushrooms, stir and cook 5 minutes longer. Stir in hot liquid and bring to a boil. Lower heat, simmer covered for 25 minutes or until all liquid is absorbed.

Variation: Add 1/2 cup grated cheese and 1/4 cup additional butter just before serving. Garnish with fresh parsley.

51

ALEXANDER VALLEY VINEYARDS CHARDONNAY

Spring Risotto

1/4 C. olive oil
Salt and fresh pepper to taste
1 lb. asparagus, tips only
2 oz. snow peas, trimmed and washed
grated parmesan cheese
1 C. Alexander Valley Vineyards Chardonnay
5 to 6 C. chicken stock, homemade if possible
1 small yellow summer squash, cut in half lengthwise and sliced

1-1/2 C. chopped leeks
2 C. Arborio rice
2 T. chopped parsley
2 ripe plum tomatoes, peeled and diced

Heat the oil in a heavy deep saucepan over medium heat. Add the leeks and salt and pepper and sauté until translucent, about 5 minutes. Add the rice and cook, stirring, another 5 minutes. At the same time bring the stock to a boil in another saucepan. Reduce the heat and keep it at a simmer.

Slowly add 1 cup of the hot stock to the rice mixture, stirring constantly, and allow it to simmer. When the liquid has been absorbed, add 1 cup of Chardonnay, stirring, and simmer until this has been absorbed. This should be a fairly even process on medium heat. Continue to add stock to the rice 1/2 cup at a time, reserving one cup at the end. This should take around 15 minutes.

Add the snow peas, squash, asparagus and tomatoes. Continue to add the remaining stock in 1/4 cup increments and stir constantly until the rice is slightly creamy. This should take about 5 minutes and the rice should be tender by this point. Serve at once, garnished with chopped parsley, freshly grated parmesan cheese, and Alexander Valley Vineyards Chardonnay.

ALEXANDER VALLEY VINEYARDS MERLOT

Vegetables a la Murphy

Almost 20 years ago Katie Wetzel Murphy attended La Varenne cooking school in Paris, France. There she learned the basics for this recipe, which she has adapted to her family's taste. A dry white wine can be substituted for the Merlot, but she likes to use Merlot because it turns the onions a lovely pink color. This dish can be prepared ahead and refrigerated, then served cold or warm. It is a wonderful appetizer or first course; it is also a delicious side dish or topping to grilled meats. The warm softness of Merlot complements the lively herb and vegetable flavors.

1/2 lb. mushrooms, quartered if large
18-20 small onions
1 C. Alexander Valley Vineyards Merlot
1 C. chicken stock
2 shallots, finely chopped
1 clove garlic, crushed
2 t. tomato paste
juice of 1 lemon
2 T. oil
1 t. coriander
bouquet garni (a tied bunch of parsley rosemary & thyme)
garnish
1 T. chopped parsley
1 lemon, thinly sliced

Pour boiling water over the onions. Let stand 2 minutes; drain and peel them. Combine the wine, stock, shallots, garlic, tomato paste, lemon juice, oil and bouquet garni in a shallow pan and simmer 5 minutes. Add the onions and simmer 10 minutes or until almost cooked. Add the mushrooms and continue simmering 3 minutes or until both vegetables are tender.

Transfer the onions and mushrooms to a glass serving bowl. Boil the cooking liquid until reduced to 1 cup. Let liquid cool, discard the bouquet garni and pour over the vegetables. Season with salt and pepper-Vegetables a la Murphy should be quite piquant. Cover and chill thoroughly; the vegetables can be prepared up to 48 hours ahead.

Just before serving, sprinkle the dish with parsley and arrange the lemon slices on top.

SAUCES

ALEXANDER VALLEY VINEYARDS
CABERNET SAUVIGNON

Cabernet Sauce

2 C. Cabernet Sauvignon
1 C. Chicken stock
1 Bay leaf
1 Rosemary sprig

3 T. Mustard, whole-grain

Combine first four ingredients in a sauce pan. Reduce this mixture by half by boiling over high heat (12-15 minutes). Remove the herbs and stir in mustard. Keep sauce warm while broiling meat (pork or Lamb loin); pour over slices. Enjoy with a glass (or two!) of Alexander Valley Vineyards Cabernet Sauvignon.

PINE RIDGE
CHENIN BLANC

Pickled Ginger Sauce (for fish)

2 T. sesame oil
3 shallots, peeled and minced
3 cloves garlic, smashed
1 T. fresh peeled ginger, grated
1 C. chicken stock
1 red bell pepper
2 T. pickled ginger

Add sesame oil to skillet. Add shallots and garlic and cook until tender. Add remaining ingredients. Cook until pepper is soft. Remove skillet from heat. Puree mixture in blender until liquid. Strain sauce to remove lumps. Can be made 1 week in advance. Do not boil when reheating.

55

SEGHESIO WINERY ZINFANDEL

Red Sauce

3 T. olive oil
8 cloves garlic, minced
1 yellow pepper, chopped
6 Roma tomatoes, chopped
1 C. Seghesio Zinfandel
1/4 C. freshbasil, chopped
1 t. capers

1 yellow onion, chopped
1 green pepper, chopped
8 - 10 mushrooms, chopped
2 - 15 oz. cans tomato puree
1/2 C. fresh Italian parsley, chopped
1 t. freshly ground pepper

Sauté onion and garlic in olive oil until onions are clear. Add peppers, mushrooms and Roma tomatoes. Sauté slowly for about 20 minutes. Stir in tomato puree, wine, parsley, basil, black pepper and capers. Simmer for 30 minutes. Serve over fresh pasta of your choice accompanied by Seghesio Zinfandel.

CAKEBREAD CELLARS SAUVIGNON BLANC

Cakebread Cellars

Singapore Satay Sauce
Makes 3/4 cup

2 T. unsalted roasted peanuts
1 clove garlic
1/4 C. top quality peanut butter
1 t. sugar
1/4 t. ground cumin
l/8 t. turmeric (optional)

1 small shallot
6 T. coconut milk
2 T. peanut oil
1/2 t. Chinese chili sauce
1/4 t. ground coriander

Mince the peanuts in a food processor and set aside. In a food processor, mince the shallot and garlic. Add all the remaining ingredients except the peanuts and process until completely smooth, about 20 seconds. If you want a little deeper color, add the turmeric and blend again. The sauce should be as thick as very rich cream. Transfer to a small container to store. Use within 3 days.

Sprinkle nuts over the sauce just before serving. Satay sauce should always be served at room temperature. If it has been refrigerated, bring to room temperature and stir vigorously. You may have to add a little peanut oil or water to thin the sauce.

PINE RIDGE
CHENIN BLANC

Soy-Ginger Glaze

This is a very simple sauce to serve with meats (such as beef, chicken or veal) OR fish (such as halibut and swordfish).

6 cloves garlic, smashed
2 C. water
4 T. cornstarch
1- 4" piece fresh peeled ginger root, grated and chopped

2 C. soy sauce
2 C. sugar

Put all ingredients except cornstarch in heavy saucepan. Mix well. Heat on low for 1 hour. Mix cornstarch with a small bit of water to make a paste and stir into above mixture to thicken. Heat sauce on low for 20 minutes. Strain sauce to remove lumps.

Can be made 5 days in advance. When reheating, do not boil mixture.

PIPER SONOMA
METHODE CHAMPENOISE-BLANC. DE NOIRS

Sparkling Citrus Marinade for Chicken or Seafood

Special thanks to John Ash of Aqua Restaurant in San Francisco for this stunning sparkling citrus marinade recipe.

4 chicken breasts or 1 lb. shrimp	2/3 C. Piper Sonoma Brut or Blanc de Noirs
1/2 apple cider	2 T. orange zest, minced
3 T. fresh orange juice	1 T. fresh lemon juice
1 T. fresh parsley, minced	1/2 t. toasted sesame oil (optional)
1 t. honey	1/2 t. salt
big pinch red pepper flakes	

Combine all ingredients in a bowl. Marinate chicken overnight (or 2 hours for shrimp), covered and refrigerated. Wipe off excess marinade before grilling or broiling. (If using shrimp, you may wrap them in fresh basil leaves and zucchini slices before grilling or broiling.) Reserve marinate for sauce.

Basil/Zucchini Wrap (optional):

1 fresh basil leaf per shrimp
1 very thin slice of zucchini per shrimp, 3" long

Blanch zucchini slices for 5 seconds in rapidly boiling water to soften. Wrap each shrimp in one basil leaf and one zucchini slice. Secure with skewer, and grill or broil.

Sauce:

1-1/2 t. cornstarch
1/4 cup Piper Sonoma Brut or Blanc de Noirs
reserved marinade

Dissolve cornstarch in wine (or water). Bring marinade to a boil and reduce to simmer. Whisk cornstarch mixture into simmering marinade and cook for 2 minutes longer to thicken slightly. Drizzle over and around cooked chicken or shrimp.

PINE RIDGE
CHENIN BLANC

Yellow Bell Pepper Sauce for Fish

2 T. sesame oil
4 cloves garlic, smashed
1 C. chicken stock
1 yellow bell pepper, chopped
salt to taste

3 shallots, peeled and minced
1-1/2 T. fresh ginger peeled and grated
2 T. rice wine vinegar
2 T. lime juice

Add sesame oil to skillet. Add shallots and garlic and cook until tender. Add remaining ingredients except lime juice and salt. Cook until pepper is soft. Remove skillet from heat. Add lime juice and salt. Puree mixture in blender until liquid. Strain sauce to remove lumps. Can be made 1 week in advance. Do not boil when reheating.

PINE RIDGE
CHENIN BLANC

Wasabi Sauce for Fish

2 T. vegetable oil
3 cloves garlic, smashed
1 green bell pepper, chopped
1 T. cilantro
1 T. wasabi powder
salt, to taste

3 shallots, peeled and minced
2 serrano chilies, minced
1 C. chicken stock

Add sesame oil to skillet. Add shallots and garlic and cook until tender. Add chilies and pepper and heat on high for 1 minute. Add chicken stock and cook on low heat until pepper is soft.

Remove pan from heat. Add cilantro and salt. Make a paste with the wasabi powder and water and add to sauce. Puree mixture in blender until liquid. Strain sauce to remove lumps.

Can be made 1 week in advance. Do not boil when reheating.

ENTREE

SEGHESIO WINERY ZINFANDEL

Chili Beans

1 can kidney beans, 6 lbs. 12 oz. size
6 C. chopped onions
15 T. chili powder
15 T. water

5 lbs. ground beef
6-2/3 C. tomato soup
5 T. flour
5 t. salt

Brown meat, remove from pan. Sauté onions. Make a paste with the chili, flour and water. Blend all ingredients together. Cook over low heat for 45 minutes, stirring often. Use less than 5 pounds ground meat if meat is served on the menu.

MC DOWELL VALLEY VINEYARDS SYRAH

Red Wine with Fish

Inspired by Julia Child and perfected by Rich Keehn. Unusual, delicious and easily multiplied for more guests. Serve with McDowell Bistro Syrah or Grenache Rose. Serves 2.

For fish filets:
1 large russet potato per 2 persons
3-4 T. olive or vegetable oil
1 T. fresh oregano or basil, minced
1/3 C. chopped leeks, julienne
1/2 C. clarified butter
2 fresh filets of fish (red snapper or other meaty fish)

4 T. sesame seed, toasted
1/3 C. red bell pepper, julienne
2 slices sourdough bread

For sauce:
1/2 C. shallots or onions, minced
1 T. each butter and olive oil
1 T. fresh parsley, minced
2 black peppercorns
2 carrots, coarsely chopped
2 C. fish or chicken stock
2 C. Mc Dowell Bistro Syrah or Grenache Rose

1 T. garlic, minced
4 T. fresh oregano or basil, minced
2 allspice berries
2 cloves
1 stalk celery or fennel, coarsely chopped
2 T. butter

Continued...

Preparation of fish fillets (First 5 steps can be done early in the day):
1.   Chop fresh herb, peel potatoes and square off sides, lengthwise. Slice potatoes length-wise, paper thin (1/8" thick) with mandolin then dip or brush both sides with light coating of oil. On sheet of wax paper, overlap potato in horizontal rows, also overlapping at center seam. Make each potato jacket about 8 inches wide by 5 inches long.

2.   Place fresh fish fillet down center seam, season with salt, fresh cracked pepper and minced herb. Bring both side-flaps of potato up and over the fillet, overlapping on the top/center seam. Trim the top and bottom to make it square. Transfer fish fillets to a cookie sheet or platter, cover completely with plastic wrap (so potato won't oxidize) and place something heavy on top to keep potato flaps in place (we use a cutting board). Refrigerate for at least 30 minutes or until ready to cook.

3.   Toast sesame seeds on cookie sheet in 375° oven for 7-10 minutes, until golden brown, shaking once or twice. Do not burn. Reserve for garnish. Clarify butter. Cut bread slices on diagonal and brush with clarified butter. Sauté until golden brown. Reserve.

4.   Trim leeks and julienne into 1 inch long pieces. Core red peppers, remove seeds and veins and julienne into 1 inch long pieces. Cover with plastic wrap and refrigerate until ready to serve.

To make the sauce:
5.   Mince shallots and garlic, chop carrots and fennel, then sauté in olive oil/butter for several minutes. Add stock and wine (or reduce wine separately) and reduce by 1/ 2 or more. Strain and reserve.

Twenty minutes before serving time:
6.   Heat large dinner plates, warm sauce and whisk in 2 Tbsp. butter to "polish", keep warm. Sauté julienned leeks and bell pepper in clarified butter, keep warm. In heavy skillet, coat pan bottom with clarified butter and fry fish fillets over medium/high heat, about 5 minutes on the first side or until potatoes are golden brown and crisp. Loosen the bottom and carefully turn over with 1 or 2 large spatulas; fry second side for 5-7 minutes or until fish has turned white and potatoes are a crispy, golden brown.

7.   On heated plate, spoon bed of sautéed leeks/red bell pepper in center, nestle fish fillet in middle, spoon sauce down each side of plate (not on fish) and garnish with toasted sesame seeds and fresh herb sprig and toast. Serve immediately with a glass of McDowell Bistro Syrah.

CLOS PEGASE
SAUVIGNON BLANC

CLOS PEGASE

Sea Bass a la Pegasus

The best treatment of fresh seafood is often the least treatment. Sea Bass at the height of its flavor is well served by the following:

4 Sea Bass steaks   l pat butter
Fresh dill, dried tarragon   Clos Pegase Sauvignon Blanc

Preheat oven to 320°. Place the bass in a baking dish. Rub the fish with butter and douse with a cup of Clos Pegase Sauvignon Blanc. Sprinkle with a mixture of finely chopped dill and dried tarragon. Salt and pepper to taste. Bake at 320° for 10 minutes per inch thickness, or until it separates to the touch. Suggested accompaniment: asparagus with hollandaise sauce and baby baked potatoes.

RENAISSANCE VINEYARDS
SAUVIGNON BLANC

Pasta with Lobster Sauce

8 live lobsters   5 shallots, minced
4 garlic cloves, minced   1/2 onion, minced
2 sticks of celery, minced   1 carrot, grated and minced
2 tomatoes, peeled, seeded, chopped   6 bay leaves
3 t. thyme   1/2-1 t. cayenne
1/4 C. Brandy   4 oz. butter
salt   Garnish with chopped parsley
Fettuccine pasta fresh if possible, for eight
2 lb. sliced butter mushrooms, sautéed separately in butter

Sauté the vegetables, except mushrooms, in the butter until soft, but not brown. Add seasonings towards the end. Add the wine and let reduce by a little more than half. Add the cream and reduce until slightly thickened. Taste for balance in seasonings. Sauce may be made ahead to this point.

Meanwhile, boil live lobsters for 8 minutes. Shell and remove tail and claw meat. Try to leave claw shells intact for garnish. Slice into bite-sized pieces. When ready to serve, heat sauce, add the sautéed mushrooms, brandy and lobster. Cook just long enough to heat. Cook pasta. Toss some sauce with the pasta. Ladle more on top and sprinkle with parsley. Garnish with the lobster claws. Serves 8-10.

HANNA WINERY
CHARDONNAY

Grilled Salmon Steaks & Pineapple Salsa

1-1/2 C. fresh pineapple, chopped
1/4 C. red onion, chopped
2 T. sugar
1 T. lemon juice
1/2 t. fresh jalapeno, chopped
1 t. fresh ginger root, grated
4 T. fresh mint, chopped

4 salmon steaks

Blend all salsa ingredients; refrigerate 4 hours before serving. Grill salmon steaks, do not overcook--rare is better. Spoon small amount of salsa on each steak. Pass the bowl of remaining salsa, serve with Hanna Chardonnay.

QUIVIRA VINEYARDS
SAUVIGNON BLANC

Grilled Salmon, Japanese style

"I learned this method of cooking salmon, from a Japanese friend, while living in Tokyo many years ago. Salmon cooked in this manner is a perfect complement to Quivira Sauvignon Blanc." -Holly Wendt

Lay a boned salmon filet, skin side down, on a piece of heavy duty foil curling up the edges to form a pan. Drizzle a small amount of lemon juice and salad oil over fish.

Grill over moderate coals with lid on barbecue (or loosely tent fish with foil) until thickest part of fish is almost opaque. The fish will continue cooking after removed from fire and must never be over cooked. (This recipe works well under oven broiler too, but the smoke flavor from the charcoal is best.)

QUIVIRA

Serve with lemon wedges or a cucumber-dill sauce:
1 part mayonnaise   1 part sour cream
a little lemon juice   dill weed
finely chopped cucumber

BUENA VISTA CHARDONNAY

Pacific Salmon Chardonnay
Serves four

2 large fresh salmon fillets
2 T. butter
3/4 C. Buena Vista Carneros Chardonnay
1/2 C. green onions, chopped
1 C. fresh button mushrooms, sliced
1/4 C. parsley, minced
1 T capers

Salt and pepper fillets. On a cookie sheet, place fish skin side down on a sheet of heavy foil large enough to fold over and cover fish completely. In a skillet, partially sauté mushrooms, parsley and onions in 1 tablespoon butter and sprinkle mixture over fish. Heat one cup Buena Vista Carneros Chardonnay and 1 more tablespoon butter and add capers. Pour wine over fish and then fold foil over salmon and seal tightly.

Bake at 350° for 25-40 minutes or until it flakes. Garnish with fresh dill weed and lemon wedges. Serve with brown rice and a glass of Buena Vista Carneros Chardonnay

KORBEL
CHAMPAGNE/BRUT

SINCE 1882

Poached Salmon with Five Minute Sauces
By Teresa Douglas-Mitchell, Culinary Director

6 - 6 to 8 oz. Salmon fillets
2 T. Butter (optional)

3 C. Korbel Brut Champagne
Salt and Pepper to taste

Walnut - Horseradish Cream:
1/2 C. Walnuts
1-1/2 C. Sour Cream

2 - 3 t. Horseradish
Salt/White Pepper to taste

Chipolte Mayonnaise:
1 - 5 oz Can Smoked Chipolte Chilies
Salt to taste

1-1/2 C. Mayonnaise

Pesto Vinaigrette:
2 C. Basil (or cilantro and mint)
3/4 C. Walnuts
1/2 C. Salad oil

4 cloves garlic
1/2 C. Extra virgin olive oil
1-1/4 C. Grated parmesan cheese

....
1/2 C. extra virgin olive oil
2 T. Balsamic Vinegar

1/4 C. Korbel Brut Champagne
Salt/Pepper to taste

To poach the salmon place it in a skillet (2 for 6 pieces of fish), season and cover partially with the champagne. Simmer over moderate heat until the fish turns from transparent to opaque (a matter of minutes, but varies depending upon the thickness). Remove from the pan, and reduce the remaining liquid, whisking in the butter at the last to form a sauce.

Or prepare one of the Five Minute Sauces:
A)   Place all the ingredients for the Walnut - Horseradish Cream in a food processor. Blend until the nuts are finely ground and season to taste.
B)   For the Chipolte Mayonnaise, puree the chilies and add them to the mayonnaise to the desired spiciness. Freeze the remaining puree for future use. Season with salt if desired.
C)   To prepare the Pesto Vinaigrette, combine the basil or other herbs, the garlic and walnuts in a food processor. Pulse the machine until the mixture is finely ground. Slowly add the olive oil, and then the cheese. Take 1/2 cup of the pesto and whisk in the remaining oil, the champagne and vinegar. Season the sauce to taste. The remaining pesto can also be frozen for future use.

PEDRONCELLI
FUME BLANC

Seared Salmon with Rice Paper & Citrus Vinaigrette

Ron Eby, a 1993 graduate, is currently working at the Hyatt Regency in Columbus. He created this appetizer and won first place as the best match with the Pedroncelli Fume Blanc.

8 sheets rice paper	8 oz. salmon
2 T. olive oil	4 T. vinegar
1 T. grated ginger	1 T. minced garlic
2 T. chopped cilantro	1 T. tomatoes, julienned
*1 T. lemon juice	1 T. red onion, diced
*1 T. orange juice	1 T. sliced plums
*1 T. lime juice	
(*cut out 2 segments for garnish)	

Deep fry rice paper until crisp. Sear salmon in a little olive oil. Set aside but keep warm. In the same pan, add rest of the olive oil and remaining ingredients to make the dressing. Place portions of the seared salmon in each of the rice paper cups. Pour over the salmon. Garnish with the lemon, lime or orange segments. Serves 8.
—Serve with Pedroncelli Dry Creek Valley Fume Blanc.

BYINGTON WINERY
FUME BLANC

Scallops L'Orange
Serves 3-4

2 T. butter
1 lb. bay scallops
10 mushroom caps
2/3 C. Byington Fume Blanc
1 C. whipping cream
salt and pepper to taste
Parmesan cheese, grated

1 T. fresh ginger, grated
1 T. lemon juice
1/2 t. frozen concentrated orange juice
fettuccini noodles, cooked and drained

Continued...

Preheat broiler. Melt the butter in a skillet; add the scallops, mushrooms and ginger. Sauté 2 minutes. Transfer to a hot platter.

Add the wine and lemon juice to the skillet, scraping up the bits in the pan. Cook and reduce by half, about 10 minutes. Blend in the cream; cook and reduce another 10 to 15 minutes. Fold the scallops and mushrooms into the cream sauce. Add the orange juice concentrate, salt, and pepper.

Place the fettuccini on an oven-proof serving platter. (Red beet noodles may be used instead of the fettuccini noodles for a variation in color and taste.) Pour the scallops and sauce over the fettuccini. Sprinkle the top with Parmesan cheese. Broil slightly to melt the cheese and serve immediately. Serve with a fresh glass of Byington Fume Blanc.

HUSCH VINEYARDS CHARDONNAY

Scallops with Papaya and Ginger Beurre Blanc
Created by Chef Alan Kantor of the MacCallum House Restaurant in Medocino to match with Husch Chardonnay.

6-1/2 oz. scallops per serving
2 shallots diced fine
1 T. ginger root, peeled & finely diced
1 C. rice wine vinegar
1 C. fish stock
12 oz. butter, cut into small pieces

ripe papaya, peeled, seeded, 1/4' diced
1 C. Husch Chardonnay
1 C. orange juice
1/4 C. cream

Sweat shallots and ginger (cook with 1 Tbsp. butter over very low heat in a sauce pan until soft). Add 1/2 of the diced papaya and continue to cook slowly for 5 minutes. Add remaining ingredients except butter, cream and 1/2 of the papaya. Reduce to one cup liquid over medium heat. Take off heat and immediately whisk in butter a few pieces at a time until smooth. Add cream. Strain. Season to taste with sea salt and white pepper. Add remaining papaya.

Quickly sear scallops in olive oil until golden brown (leave slightly raw in middle). Serve immediately.

FOREST HILL VINEYARD CHARDONNAY

Sunshine Scallops
Serves 4

3 T. fresh lemon juice
1-1/2 t. fine julienne of fresh ginger root
1-1/2 t. oriental sesame oil
3/4 lb. sea scallops, halved to make two mini 'pancakes'

1-1/2 t. cornstarch
salt to taste
1-1/2 T. fresh orange juice

For sauce, stir together the first grouping. Dredge scallops in additional cornstarch, and fry in light oil in skillet for a few minutes only (about 2 minutes each side until golden). Stir in sauce and bring to boil. Serve with Forest Hill Vineyard Private Reserve Napa Valley Chardonnay.

HEITZ CELLAR CHARDONNAY

Citrus & Apricot Prawns
By Kathleen Heitz

12 large prawns
2-3 T. olive oil
1 T. fresh ginger, finely chopped
1/2 cup fresh scallions, chopped
2 T. fresh parsley, finely chopped
1 T. white wine
1 T. fresh chives, chopped
juice of 1/2 lime
juice of 1/2 orange
juice of 1 lemon
3 T. Grand Marnier Liqueur
2 T. candied ginger, finely chopped

zest the rind of:
1/2 lemon
1/2 orange
1/2 lime

Continued...

1/2 C. dried apricots, cut into thin strips
1 C. papaya (or mango or nectarines), diced
2 T. fresh scallions, chopped
1 T. fresh parsley, chopped

Wash the prawns, removing the shell but leaving the tail on, and deveining. Place on a plate and pat dry with a paper towel. In a saucepan heat the olive oil and add the fresh ginger, scallions, and parsley. Sauté until the scallions are soft and then add the prawns, wine and chives and continue to stir. As the prawns begin to turn pink in color, add the lemon, lime and orange juice along with the Grand Marnier and candied ginger. Let simmer for a minute or two while adding the three citrus rinds. Remove from heat and refrigerate.

Remove the prawns from the refrigerator and add the dried apricots and papaya and toss mixture. Sprinkle some fresh scallions and parsley for color.

CUVAISON
MERLOT

Curried Crepes Filled with Sea Bass and Rock Prawns on a Merlot Beurre Rouge
By Chef Jeffrey Allen Young

Curried Crepes:
1 C. milk
3/4 C. flour
1/4 t. salt
3 eggs
2 t. curry powder

In a mixing bowl, whisk together milk, eggs, flour, curry powder and salt. Let batter rest for 30 minutes. Use a 6" pan to make the crepes.

Filling for Crepes:
1 lb. sea bass
4 oz. mushrooms, sliced
fish stock
8 oz. rock prawns
1 C. thick white sauce

Lightly poach Sea Bass and Rock Prawns in a little fish stock. Sauté mushrooms in a little butter until slightly limp. Remove from heat. Combine fish, white sauce, and mushrooms in a bowl and fold together gently.

Continued...

70

To assemble, place 3/4 cup of filling on one half of the crepe. Fold crepe in half and then quarters. Place crepes in a baking dish. Cover with foil and bake at 350° for thirty minutes.

Merlot Beurre Rouge:

2 C. Cuvaison Merlot
1 Jalapeno pepper, whole
1/2 C. Whipping Cream
salt and pepper

1 T. Red wine vinegar
2 Jalapeno peppers, finely minced
1-1/2 sticks butter

Combine first four ingredients in sauce pan. Bring to a boil. Reduce to one cup. Add cream and reduce again to 3/4 cup. Using a blender or hand mixer, add butter, salt and pepper.

Presentation:

Place one crepe on each plate with julienned vegetable and fresh watercress. Drizzle the Buerre Rouge over the crepe and form a little mound of the same next to the crepe.

Serve with Cuvaison Merlot. Bon Appetit

DRY CREEK VINEYARDS CHARDONNAY

Fillet of Sole in Tarragon Orange Butter
By Brad Wallace

4 T. butter
1/2 lb. mushrooms, sliced
1 small onion, chopped
1 lb. sole, 4 fillets, washed and patted dry
1/4 C. Dry Creek Chardonnay
1/4 C. orange juice
1/2 t. dried tarragon
salt & ground pepper to taste

Preheat oven to 350°. Melt 2 Tbsp. butter in a skillet over medium-high heat. Add mushrooms and onions. Sauté until softened, about 7 minutes. Place fillets in an oven-proof dish, pour the wine and orange juice over fillets. Dot each fillet with the remaining butter. Sprinkle with tarragon, salt and pepper. Spoon the mushroom-onion mixture evenly over each fillet. Cover with foil and bake until done, about 25 minutes. Serve with Dry Creek Vineyards Chardonnay.

FETZER VINEYARDS
CHARDONNAY

Grilled Brook Trout with Pumpkin Sauce

Michael Foley is a third-generation restaurateur whose years of experience are evident at his highly-regarded Printer's Row and nearby Foley's restaurants in Chicago. Foley cherishes local products, and he has been instrumental in nurturing relationships with heartland producers to access the regions best.

1/4 C. onion, chopped
1/4 C. leek, rinsed, chopped white part only
1/4 C. celery, chopped
1 T. butter
2 C. pumpkin puree, fresh or unseason canned
1/8 t. cinnamon, ground
1 clove garlic, ground
1/8 t. nutmeg
1/8 t. allspice
1 sprig fresh thyme (or 1/2 t. dried)
1 bay leaf
1 C. Fetzer Chardonnay
1 qt. fish stock (or 1/2 quart clam juice & 1/2 water)
1/2 C. heavy whipping cream
1/2 C. creme fraiche
8 boneless brook trout (approx. 12 oz. ea.)

Sauté vegetables in butter until tender, approximately 5 minutes. Add pumpkin puree, spices and herbs. Cook 5 minutes over medium heat. Add wine, bring to boil, reduce over low-medium heat for 15-20 minutes, stirring occasionally, until thick. Add stock, simmer 10-15 minutes. Slowly add cream while stirring constantly. Reduce over medium heat for 10 minutes. Salt and pepper to taste.

Brush trout with olive oil, salt and pepper, and grill for 5-7 minutes, or until done, or bake in a 375° oven for 7 minutes. Fold creme fraiche into reduced sauce. Nap each trout with 2 Tbsp. of sauce, and serve immediately with Fetzer Chardonnay.

SHAFER VINEYARDS
CHARDONNAY

Walnut Encrusted Trout

4 whole Trout	1/4 C. Flour
2 large eggs	2 T. water
3/4 C. walnuts, toasted	1/4 C. Oil
6 oz. Pasta	1 T. Shallots, fine chop
1-1/2 t. Garlic, fine chop	1 T. Olive oil
1 C. White wine	2/3 C. Clam juice
1 C. heavy cream	1 T. Parsley, chopped
2 T. Butter	Salt to taste
White pepper	
1 ea. Red and yellow bell pepper, roasted, skinned & seeded	

Sauce:
Reduce cream by half, set aside. Cut bell peppers into 1/2" diamonds. Heat oil in skillet and sauté shallots and garlic. Add wine and reduce to almost evaporated. Add clam juice and reduce by half. Whisk in cream and add bell peppers. Season and whisk in butter.

Trout:
Remove fins, head and tail from trout. Scale fish, remove its backbone (or have the butcher do so), and cut out pin bones. In food processor, chop walnuts to a mealy texture. Season flour and beat eggs with the water. Dust the trout patting off excess flour, dredge through eggwash and press skin side into walnut meal. Over a medium flame heat oil and place walnut side down. Fry until golden brown and flip. Cooking time should be about 5 minutes.

Assembly:
Before cooking trout, cook pasta in well salted water. Drain and coat with 3/4 of sauce. Mound pasta in center of plate. Remove trout from pan and pat with paper towel to remove excess grease. Place on top of pasta and ladle about 2 Tbsp. of sauce on top. Garnish with parsley and a thin slice of lemon.

GROTH VINEYARDS & WINERY
CABERNET SAUVIGNON

Filets with Groth Cabernet

1/2 lb. mushrooms quartered
3 T. butter
salt & fresh ground pepper to taste
3 T. green onions, minced
6 filets steaks wrapped in bacon
2 T. butter
1 T. olive oil

Sauté mushrooms and onions in butter and set aside. Dry the steaks and wrap the bacon around them, securing with a string. Sear the filets in the hot butter and oil. Reduce heat and sauté until done to taste. Add salt and discard the bacon. Set on platter in warm oven.

To skillet add:
1/2 C. beef stock   1 T. tomato paste
1/4 C. Groth Cabernet Sauvignon

Reduce liquid by half. Thicken with 3 Tbsp. cornstarch dissolved in water. Add the mushrooms and heat. Pour over the filets and serve garnished with 2 tsp. of chopped fresh thyme or parsley. Serve with Groth Cabernet Sauvignon.

ST. SUPERY
CABERNET SAUVIGNON

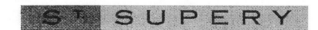

Flank Steak Extraordinaire

1/2 lb. flank steak   1/2 C. soy sauce
3-4 T. olive oil   chives, finely chopped
coarse ground black pepper

Make small cross-grain cuts on the top length of the flank steak, 1" apart. Sprinkle top with chives and black pepper. Add soy sauce. Let soak at least 2 hours in the 'fridge. Heat up a heavy skillet. Add olive oil and slab of beef (uncut side down). Cooking time depends on the thickness of the meat. Sear the outside and keep the inside moist; rare to medium rare. Generally, 10 minutes for the bottom and 5 minutes for the top, sliced side. When done, remove onto carving board and slice cross-grain, 1/3" thick. Dish onto a warm plate.

MURPHY-GOODE WINERY
CABERNET SAUVIGNON

Irish Stew

1-1/2 lbs cubed Round Steak
3 onions, chopped
2 green peppers, chopped
1 t. Beau Monde
1 sprig parsley, chopped
8 carrots - cut to size desired

1-1/2 lbs cubed Lamb
3 C. celery, chopped
4 cloves garlic, chopped
1 t. dill weed
1 C. beef stock
8 potatoes - cut to size desired

Roll meat in flour. Brown in olive oil. Remove meat and lightly sauté onions, celery, green peppers and garlic. Place in stock pot, and beef stock and seasonings. Cook slowly for about 2 hours. Add carrots and potatoes and cook 1 hour more. (Can add 1 cup of Lager or Guinness or water as needed.) Thicken with flour, corn starch or corn meal if desired. Salt and pepper as needed. Serve with Murphy-Goode Cabernet Sauvignon.

SANFORD WINERY
PINOT NOIR

New York Steak Arugula
Created Especially By Shirley Sarvis.

1 prime and well-aged New York steak, cut 1-1/2 inches thick (about 1 pound), trimmed of all outside fat (to yield about 12 ounces lean beef)
Salt (preferably coarse)
Freshly ground premium quality white pepper
Arugula salad (recipe below)

Wipe meat dry. Season well with salt and pepper. Let stand for 1 hour or longer in order to reach room temperature. Heat a medium-sized heavy frying pan over medium-high heat until hot. Sprinkle lightly with salt. Add meat and brown well on one side; turn and brown on second side; continue to cook, lowering heat if necessary and turning occasionally as necessary in order to get the brownness and doneness you wish, about 4 to 5 minutes total for rare. (Add a little olive oil if needed to prevent sticking.) Remove from pan and let stand for about 2 minutes.

Continued...

Very thinly slice across the grain. Arrange slices, slightly overlapping and with all carving juices over, on two slightly warm serving plates. Side with salad. Makes 2 generous servings .

Arugula Salad:
Gently turn 2 to 3 cups (loosely pack to measure) small leaves (not stems) of young very fresh arugula with enough very fresh light olive oil to cloak well, and with salt and freshly ground premium-quality white pepper to season well.

This makes a sumptuous little supper: The fine steak slices, the lifted arugula salad, freshly fried very thinly sliced potatoes (a threesome on one plate), and the 1986 Pinot Noir. The wine carries enough spirit of youth to mingle compatibly and hold its presence with the true, fine and uncluttered tastes of steak, salad and potatoes. You can combine the steak and salad into eating bites.

To prepare fresh fried potatoes:
Slice unpeeled little red potatoes as thinly as possible (cucumber slicer is suitable). Put into a heavy frying pan with generous unsalted butter barely bubbling over medium heat (or use light olive oil)--in barely more than a single layer. Turn when lightly golden on bottom and cook to goldenness and crispness to your taste. Season with salt.

BANDIERA
CABERNET SAUVIGNON

Savory Steaks with Sun-Dried Tomato Topping

4 - 8 oz. steaks
1/2 C. parsley, chopped
1 T. salt

3 cloves garlic
2 T. olive oil
2 t. black pepper

Combine all ingredients in a small bowl. Rub each steak on both sides with mixture. Let stand 20 minutes in refrigerator. Grill to desired doneness.

Sun-Dried Tomato Topping:

1/4 C. sun dried tomatoes, chopped
2 t. fresh oregano, chopped
1/2 t. ground black pepper
1/4 C. sliced stale french bread, remove crust and cut in 1/2 inch cubes
1/2 C. sliced stale french bread, remove crust and crumble into small pieces
2 cloves garlic, chopped OR 1 t. garlic powder

1 t. salt
2 T. olive oil

Toss all ingredients together in a mixing bowl. Spread in a thin layer on a cookie sheet. Place in a 300° oven for 5 minutes. Stir and return to oven for 5 minutes. Repeat this process until crumbs are toasted. Serve at room temperature over steaks. Delicious with Bandiera Cabernet Sauvignon.

HANNA WINERY
CABERNET SAUVIGNON

Steak & Mushrooms a' la Hanna

4 steaks, your favorite cut
2 C. mushrooms, chopped
2 T. olive oil
handful of Italian parsley, chopped

2 Maui onions, chopped
2 cloves garlic
1 C. Hanna Cabernet Sauvignon
salt and pepper

Heat olive oil, sauté onion until soft. Add wine, reduce for 10 minutes. Add mushrooms and sauté until soft. Add parsley. Grill steaks until just done and pour sauce over steaks and serve immediately with Hanna Cabernet Sauvignon.

CLOS PEGASE
CABERNET SAUVIGNON

CLOS PEGASE

Tataki Fillet

1 piece (1 to 1-1/2 lb.) fat-trimmed beef tenderloin
3 T. soy sauce
3 T. olive oil
1 C. thinly sliced green onions

Mix meat with soy and 1 tablespoon of the oil. Cover and chill at least 30 minutes or until the next day.

Cook meat on a grill 4 to 6 inches above a solid bed of medium-hot coals (you can hold your hand at grill level only 3 to 4 seconds) just until very rare (cut to test), about 15 minutes; turn to brown evenly. Put meat on a platter and keep warm in a 150° oven up to 30 minutes. Or, if made ahead, cover and chill until the next day. Just before serving, slice meat. Also place a 10- to 12-inch frying pan on high heat. Add remaining oil; when hot, add onions. Stir just until slightly wilted, about 30 seconds. Spoon over meat.

CAKEBREAD CELLARS
ZINFANDEL

Cakebread Cellars

Wild Boar Ribs with Robert's Secret Barbecue Sauce

Wild Boar Ribs

Robert's Secret Barbecue Sauce:

1 C. onion, minced
1/4 C. vegetable oil
1/4 C. water
1/4 C. lemon juice
2 T. Dijon mustard

2 cloves garlic, minced
1 C. tomato sauce
1/4 C. brown sugar
3 T. Worcestershire sauce
salt and pepper

Trim ribs of any excess fat and roast in 300° oven for 1 hour or more until tender. Sauté onion and garlic in heavy bottom saucepan until soft. Stir in the rest of the ingredients except for the salt and pepper and simmer for 20-30 minutes. Season with salt and pepper and remove from the heat. Grill ribs over a hot fire, basting with barbecue sauce. Cut ribs into portions and enjoy with a glass of Cakebread Cellars Zinfandel.
(Can order ribs from: Broken Arrow Ranch at 1-800-962-4263, and they will ship overnight).

RENAISSANCE VINEYARDS CABERNET SAUVIGNON

Arroz con Pollo

16 chicken thighs
2 onions, diced medium fine
1-1/2 C. of pearl rice
1 bottle Renaissance Cabernet Sauvignon

2 C. chicken broth
1/2 t. cinnamon
1/2 t. nutmeg
salt
black pepper

Pour wine into a saucepan. Let simmer and reduce by 1/2. Combine with the chicken broth. Meanwhile sauté chicken thighs in a large casserole pot, seasoning with salt and pepper until golden brown on both sides. Set aside.

Pour out most of the fat and sauté the onions until golden brown. Stirring constantly, add the rice and sauté until it turns opaque. Add the nutmeg, cinnamon, 1-1/2 tsp. salt, +1/2 tsp. black pepper. Then add about 3 cups of the wine mixture. Set the sautéed chicken on top of the rice in a single layer if possible. Bring liquid to a boil, cover casserole with a lid and place in a preheated 350° oven.

In one-half hour, check the rice to see if more liquid is needed. Add another cup of the wine mixture. Check again every 15 minutes or so, gradually adding more liquid as needed.

Total cooking time: 1 hour to 1 1/4 hours. Chicken will get tender and the rice will have absorbed the liquid. Serves 8. Good with sautéed zucchini.

QUIVIRA VINEYARDS
CABERNET SAUVIGNON

Balinese Chicken

1/4 C. creamy style peanut butter
3 T. soy sauce
1/2 t. pepper
1/2 t. cayenne
2 cloves garlic, finely minced
2 lbs. chicken breasts, cut into 1/2 inch cubes

1-1/2 T. lemon juice
1-1/2 t. cumin
1-1/2 t. salt
1 T. brown sugar
1 large onion, finely minced
8 - 12 inch skewers

Marinate chicken in marinade for several hours. Soak skewers in water several hours. Thread chicken on skewers. Grill 8-10 minutes over moderately hot coals or until cooked through.

J. FRITZ WINERY
MELON

Chicken Dijon with Cracked Pepper & Herb Sauce

Jay & Barbara's favorite chicken recipe. A light, but richly flavored, chicken dish. Serve with garlic mashed potatoes, steamed asparagus, plus a crisp and fruity white wine. We enjoy the J. Fritz Melon (pronounced muh lawn) as a perfect companion to this elegant dish.

8 chicken breasts—boneless-skinless halves
5 shallots, coarsely chopped
4 t. black peppercorns, cracked
5 fresh sprigs rosemary, OR 1/2 t dried
2 C. chicken stock
1 T. yellow mustard seeds
1/2 t. whole thyme, freshly minced

2 T. butter, unsalted
5 mushrooms, large quarters
1 C. J. Fritz Melon wine
5 fresh sprigs thyme, OR 1/2 t dried
1/4 C. Dijon mustard

Continued...

Melt 1 Tbsp. butter in heavy skillet over medium-high heat. Add shallots, mushrooms, and 1 tsp. pepper. Sauté until vegetables brown—about 7-8 minutes. Add J. Fritz Melon and bring to a boil; add rosemary and thyme sprigs and simmer 5 minutes. Add stock; increase heat to medium-high, boiling until liquid is reduced to 3/4 cup—about 20 minutes. Strain into saucepan. Preheat broiler or grill. Sprinkle remaining 3 tsp. pepper over both sides of chicken. Grill until cooked through, about 4-5 minutes per side. Transfer to baking sheet, brush with Dijon mustard, and sprinkle with mustard seeds. Broil until brown—about 2 minutes. Meanwhile, simmer sauce; add minced thyme and remaining 1 Tbsp. butter; whisk until melted. Spoon herb sauce over chicken and serve. Serves 4.

CHALK HILL WINERY
CHARDONNAY

Chicken with Tomatoes and White Wine Sauce

5 boneless skinless chicken breasts halves	3 T. butter
2 T. olive oil	1 T. fresh rosemary, chopped
2 cloves garlic, crushed	2 T. chopped shallots
1 - 14 oz. can plump Italian tomatoes	12 oz. fresh mushrooms, quartered
1/2 C. chicken broth	3/4 C. Chalk Hill Chardonnay
Salt & pepper to taste	

Heat butter and oil in large skillet and brown flattened chicken breast. Season with salt, pepper and chopped rosemary. Remove chicken from skillet and keep warm. In remaining oil, sauté garlic & shallots; add mushrooms and tomatoes and cook 5 minutes. Add chicken broth and Chalk Hill wine; cook sauce for 10 minutes. When it has reduced, return the chicken to the skillet and let it absorb the flavor for 3 minutes. Transfer chicken to warm place and serve with tomato sauce. Serves 6

CHALK HILL
W I N E R Y

SANFORD WINERY
SAUVIGNON BLANC

Cumin Chicken with Green Olive Salsa

Created especially by Shirley Sarvis. Garnish with parsley sprigs and accompany with boiled little new potatoes (they take nicely to the olive salsa), and follow with a mild butter lettuce salad. Fresh orange is nice for dessert.

Marinated chicken breasts (recipe below)
About 3 T. light olive oil
Green olive salsa (below)

Marinated chicken breasts:
Wipe dry 2 medium-large frying chicken breasts which have been split, boned and skinned (about 1 pound meat). Place each breast piece between two sheets of waxed paper, and pat with a meat pounder until breast is evenly 5/8 inch thick. Sprinkle with 1 teaspoon salt, 1 tablespoon ground cumin and 1 teaspoon paprika, and let stand for 5 to 10 minutes. Sprinkle with 4 teaspoons cornstarch and 4 teaspoons light olive oil, turn to mix, and let stand for 20 minutes. Fold in 1 unbeaten egg white, and let stand for 30 minutes.

Heat oil in a large heavy frying pan over medium heat. Add breasts and cook just until opaque nearly to center and golden on both sides, about 5 minutes total. Remove to slightly warm serving plates. Spoon part of salsa over. Pass remaining salsa. Makes 4 servings.

Green Olive Salsa:

Stir together 1/2 cup very fresh light olive oil, 3/16 teaspoon crushed dried hot red peppers, 6 large cloves garlic, peeled and split. Let stand for 20 minutes. Remove garlic. Stir in 3/16 teaspoon salt, 3/4 cup finely chopped pitted green olives, 3/4 teaspoon fresh lemon juice and 2 tablespoons finely chopped parsley (preferably flat-leaf (Italian).

EBERLE WINERY
CABERNET SAUVIGNON

Gary Eberle's Paella

This is Gary Eberle's most requested dish by family, staff and friends. It goes great with Eberle Cabernet Sauvignon. Serves 10-12.

1/4 C. olive oil
1 large onion
2 C. uncooked rice
3 t. salt
1 T. paprika
1/4 t. saffron
1-1/2 lb. sea scallops
24 oz. tomatoes, chopped plus juice from cans
1 1/2 lb. sausage - beef, pork, or any combination
24 oz. artichoke hearts, quarter
1/2 t. crushed red pepper, another 1/2 if desired
1 small jar pimientos, or cooked red bell peppers
1 large can, large pitted black olives
1 C. Eberle Cabernet Sauvignon

1/2 lb. boneless chicken in bite size pieces
1/4 C. water
3 cloves garlic, chopped
1/2 T. chicken bouillon
3/4 t. pepper
1-1/2 lb. cleaned shrimp
16 oz. frozen peas

Heat oil in large stock pot. Cook chicken in oil about 10 minutes, remove chicken. Cook onion and garlic in oil until onion is transparent. Stir in water, wine, tomatoes, bouillon, and all spices. Heat to boiling. Add chicken, shrimp, scallops and sausage. Simmer 15 minutes. Add more wine or water as needed.

As other ingredients are cooking, cook 2 cups of rice in separate pot. When cooked, drain and hold. Stir peas and artichoke hearts into pot. Add about 3/4 of the rice and simmer for 5 minutes. If desired add more rice for a drier dish. Serve in a paella dish or shallow baking dish. Garnish with pimento or peppers and black olives and serve with Eberle Cabernet Sauvignon.

BANDIERA
CHARDONNAY

Grilled Breast of Chicken with Orange-Apricot Glaze

4 Chicken breasts

1/2 C. apricot preserves
1/4 C. orange juice
1 clove garlic, finely chopped   1 T. ginger finely chopped
1/2 t. ground black pepper   1/2 t. salt

Combine all ingredients in a small saucepan. Stir over medium heat until preserves are melted and all ingredients are combined.

Grill the chicken breasts over medium-hot coals for about 20 minutes. Cook for 10 more minutes, brushing with glaze four times while cooking. Delicious with rice, steamed asparagus and Bandiera Chardonnay.

SEGHESIO WINERY
SAUVIGNON BLANC

Seghesio

Italian Chicken

3 T. flour   1/2 t. freshly ground pepper
3 - 4 cloves of garlic, minced   2 T. olive oil
1/4 C. fresh parsley, chopped   1 T. fresh oregano, chopped or 1 t. dried
1 T. fresh basil, chopped or 1 t. dried   1 C. Seghesio Sauvignon Blanc
Salt and pepper to taste   1 loaf sourdough French bread
1 - 3 lb. chicken, cut in pieces, or 4 chicken breasts

Dredge chicken in flour and pepper, set aside. Sauté garlic in olive oil for 3 minutes. Add floured chicken and brown both sides. When chicken is browned, add herbs and wine to pan. Simmer mixture until chicken is tender, about 20 - 30 minutes. If needed, add more wine during cooking so chicken is surrounded by liquid.

Serve chicken with sourdough French bread, using bread to absorb the flavorful broth. Seghesio Sauvignon Blanc is a perfect accompaniment to this dish.

DRY CREEK VINEYARDS
FUME BLANC

Parmesan Walnut Chicken with Mustard Sauce
By Brad Wallace

1/2 C. fresh parmesan cheese, grated
1/3 C. walnut pieces
1/3 C. all-purpose flour
salt and pepper to taste
3/4 C. onion, chopped
1/4 C. milk

1/2 C. milk
4 T. olive oil
5 T. dijon mustard
1/8 C. Dry Creek Fume Blanc

4 half chicken breasts, boned and skinned, pounded slightly

Process cheese, walnuts, and flour in food processor until nuts are finely chopped. Transfer to sheet of wax paper. Pour 1/2 cup milk into shallow dish. Pat chicken dry with paper towel. Sprinkle each breast with salt and pepper, then coat each piece with cheese mixture; dip chicken breast in milk and coat again with cheese mixture. Heat oil in skillet. Sauté breasts on both sides until golden and done, about 5 minutes. Remove breasts from pan; keep warm. Add onions to skillet and sauté until tender. Then add mustard, milk, and wine; mix well and heat thoroughly. Pour sauce over chicken. Serves four. Enjoy with Dry Creek Vineyard Fume Blanc.

OAK RIDGE VINEYARDS
WHITE ZINFANDEL

Roast Chicken Royal

2 frying chickens, quartered
1/2 C. chicken stock, (canned if necessary)
1 C. fresh mushrooms, sliced
1/4 C. fresh parsley, finely chopped

2 C. Oak Ridge Vineyards White Zinfandel
1/2 C. green onions, thinly sliced
1/2 C. celery
salt & pepper

Wash chicken quarters; while still damp sprinkle with salt and pepper. Place skin-side down in shallow baking pan; bake 15 minutes in a 425° oven. Combine remaining ingredients; pour over chicken. Bake 30 minutes longer, basting several times. Reduce heat to 350°, turn chicken skin-side up and bake another 15-30 minutes until chicken is browned. Degrease drippings and serve as gravy over chicken.

IRON HORSE VINEYARDS
PINOT NOIR

Roast Chicken with Lemon and Olives

Salt and pepper to taste
1 bunch thyme
2 lemons cut in half
1 T. olive oil
One "Rocky Sr." (large, free range roasting chicken), 4-1/2 lbs
1 C. of olives (Nicoise, Galamata or Picholine)

Preheat oven to 450°. Wash the chicken inside and out and dry thoroughly. Season the cavity with salt and pepper. Place the thyme and lemon inside the chicken, and rub with olive oil. Truss the chicken, and place the bird breast side down on roasting pan on upper rack of oven. Cook for 45 minutes and then turn breast side up, lower heat to 350°, and cook for an additional 15 minutes, basting with cooking juices. Remove from oven, carve chicken and serve with savory juices. Scatter olives over platter.

Rocky the Free Range Chicken is a Sonoma phenomenon. There are Rocky Juniors and Rocky Seniors. Both are marked with a little metal tag like Poulard de Bresse.

Wine Notes:
The Pinot Noir will go with the rest of the meal all the way through to dessert. Young Pinot Noir is generally fruity and spicy. We figure five to six glasses a bottle.

FROG'S LEAP
CHARDONNAY

Roasted Chicken

Roasted chicken is a simple, delicious cornerstone to many meals at the Williams' household. Adjust the seasonings and side dishes to the tastes of your friends or young family! Serves 4-6.

4 lbs. roasting chicken (we use a "Rocky Range" for flavor)
Fresh Rosemary or Tarragon, garlic cloves
Sea salt & pepper
Lemon
1 bottle Frog's Leap Chardonnay

Heat oven to 350°. To prepare chicken, remove excess fat from the cavity, coarsely chop about 2-3 tsp. (discard the balance). In an oven-proof pan, place the fat, 4-6 smashed cloves of garlic and 1/2 cup of wine; place the pan in the oven to heat for about 15 minutes.

Meanwhile, use your fingers to loosen the skin over the breast of the chicken and stuff each area with one to two sprigs of herb. Chop the lemon into quarters, place inside chicken cavity with 3-4 sprigs of herb and salt and pepper to taste. Truss the chicken.

Remove the pan from the oven, place the trussed chicken on its side to brown, basting, and roast for 6 minutes. Turn on its back and roast 50 minutes until tender. Add additional wine if necessary to continue basting every 10-15 minutes.

Remove from oven and untie to cool.

Note: Rich Napa Valley Carneros Chardonnay has the delicious complexity to complement poultry and enhance the subtle lemon and herb flavors that infuse this roast.

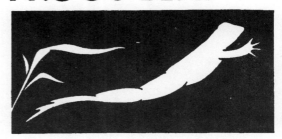

FROG'S LEAP

87

PINE RIDGE
CHENIN BLANC

PINE RIDGE
WINERY

Sa-Teh on Skewers

1 lb. boneless chicken (beef or pork can be substituted)
Cut chicken into thin 2" strips.

3 T. oil
3 cloves garlic
1 T. curry powder
1 t. fish sauce OR 1/4 teaspoon salt

1 stalk lemon grass (if available)
1/2 t. dried chili flakes
1 t. sugar or honey

In a food processor or blender combine oil, lemon grass, garlic, chili flakes, curry powder sugar and fish sauce; blend until smooth. Pour over chicken; marinate for 2 hours or overnight.

Bamboo Skewers:
Soak bamboo skewers in water. Thread meat onto skewer and barbecue or broil, tuning occasionally, until cooked. Serve with Sa-teh sauce.

Sa-teh Sauce:
1/4 C. oil
1 medium red onion, chopped
1 t. grated lime rind
1 T. fresh lemon grass, chopped (if available)

2 garlic cloves, peeled and minced
1/2 t. chili powder
1/2 t. curry powder

Heat oil in a skillet to medium-high heat. Sauté garlic, onion, chili powder, lime rind curry powder, and lemon grass for 2 - 3 minutes.

1 C. coconut milk
1/4 t. ground cinnamon
1 T. fish sauce OR 1/4 teaspoon salt
3 T. lemon juice

1/2 C. milk
2 t. tamarind paste
3 t. dark brown sugar
1 C. chunky peanut butter

Stir in remaining ingredients; mix well. Reduce heat and cook, stirring frequently until sauce thickens, about 30 minutes. Be very careful sauce does not stick to bottom of pan. Allow to cool to room temperature before serving.

MIRASSOU
BRUT CHAMPAGNE

Steamed Chicken Breasts Stuffed with Red Pepper Mousse in Champagne Sauce

Red Bell Pepper Mousse:

2 T. olive oil

1/2 t. dried thyme, crumbled

1 t. salt

1/4 C. heavy cream

2 chicken breasts halves, skinned & boned

1 clove garlic, chopped

1/4 t. white pepper

1 egg white

3 medium red bell peppers, seeded & sliced

Place a large sauté pan over medium-high heat. Add oil, peppers, garlic, and thyme. Sauté, stirring often, until peppers are limp and have lost some moisture. Set aside to cool. Cut chicken breasts into small pieces. Place in a food processor with cooled peppers, salt, and pepper. Process about 20 seconds. With processor running, slowly add egg white and cream. Scrape sides of bowl and process until all ingredients are well mixed. Chill if not using immediately.

Chicken Breasts and Champagne Sauce:

6 chicken breast halves, skinned and boned

2 shallots, sliced (or 1/4 chopper onion)

1 C. Mirassou Brut Champagne

1 C. heavy cream

1 recipe red bell pepper mousse

1 C. sliced fresh mushrooms

1 C. unsalted chicken stock

salt & pepper to taste

Place each chicken breast between two pieces of plastic wrap and pound until meat is about 1/4" thick all over. Spoon mousse onto one side of the chicken, leaving 1-1/2" boarder at edges. Fold chicken in half over the mousse and press edges of meat together. Season with salt and white pepper. Place seam side down in oiled steamed for 8 minutes.

Sauce:

Combine shallots, mushrooms, and champagne in saucepan. Boil until 2 Tbsp. liquid remain. Add chicken stock and continue boiling until sauce is reduced by half. Add cream. Boil until sauce reaches desired consistency. Pour through fine strainer and season to taste with salt and white pepper.

To serve, slice each breast diagonally and arrange slices in a half circle on heated plate. Spoon sauce over slices. Serve with Mirassou Brut Champagne.

MURPHY-GOODE WINERY
SAUVIGNON BLANC

MURPHY-GOODE
E S T A T E   W I N E R Y

Thai Grilled Chicken

Adapted from a recipe by Vorachoon Uuchinda and Narin Cotipanang of Lemongrass Restaurant in Bangkok, by Mary Lannin, Murphy-Goode Estate Winery. Serves 8.

16 Boneless chicken thighs
8 Stalks of lemongrass, cleaned and coarsely chopped
12 Green onions, coarsely chopped
1/2 C. Thai fish sauce
2/3 C. sugar
1/2 C. raw peanuts, deep fried and coarsely chopped
3 T. Sugar
1 t. Salt
8 Green onion, thinly sliced

Make the marinade by adding lemon grass (use only bottom 1/3) and green onion to food processor and finely chop; add fish sauce and sugar and stir to dissolve; marinate thighs at least three hours; grill over your favorite hardwood fire until done; garnish with green onions and peanuts that have been tossed with the sugar and salt.

SANFORD WINERY
PINOT NOIR

SANFORD

Dijon Duck Breasts

Created Especially by Shirley Sarvis. Garnish with watercress, accompany with peeled little new potatoes, lightly browned to finish, and French-cut fresh green beans.

1 whole boneless duck breast, skin and membrane removed (breast from 5-pound Petaluma or Long Island duckling), split
Salt and freshly ground premium quality white pepper
About 1 t. each light olive oil and unsalted butter
1-1/2 T. soft unsalted butter
3/4 t. Dijon-style mustard
3/4 t. brandy
2 T. dry white table wine
1/2 C. lean beef broth or stock

Continued...

Trim excess fat from breasts. If necessary to make each breast piece evenly 5/8 inch thick, place between two sheets of waxed paper and pat with a meat pounder. Season breasts well with salt and pepper. Cover loosely and let stand for 1 hour. Beat soft butter and mustard together with a fork; mix in brandy. Heat a medium-sized heavy frying pan over medium-high to high heat. When hot, add the 1 teaspoon oil and butter and heat until butter foams, then begins to stop foaming. Add breasts. Cook until well browned on one side, turn and brown on second side (lower heat and turn about two times as necessary until breast is rosy on the inside, about 3 to 4 minutes total; make a small cut in breast to check doneness; do not crowd in pan). Remove and let stand for about 4 minutes.

Meantime, remove any excess fat and burned drippings from pan; leave brown drippings. Add wine and cook and stir until reduced to 1/2 Tablespoon. Add broth and cook and stir over high heat until reduced to a scant 3 Tablespoons. Remove from heat and let cool for a moment. Carve breasts, across the grain and slightly diagonally, top to bottom, into 3/8 inch thick slices; arrange, with juices, overlapping, on slightly warm serving plates. Whisk mustard butter into pan liquid; pour over breasts. Makes 2 servings.

Variation: Also excellent with Sanford Pinot Noir is Dijon Beef Steaks. Follow recipe above except instead of duck breasts, use 1 aged New York steak (preferably prime grade), cut 1-1/4 inches thick, trimmed of all outside fat (to yield about 9 ounces lean beef), cut in half (near room temperature). Cook steaks about 3 to 4 minutes total for rare. Do not carve. Pour mustard butter over.

RENAISSANCE VINEYARDS
CABERNET SAUVIGNON

Roast Duckling with Green Peppercorn Sauce

Rinse the duckling inside and out with water; pat dry. Remove neck and excess skin flap if still attached and pull out any fat deposits found inside near the tail end.

Stuff the cavity with several whole carrot and celery sticks, broken in half; this helps the shape of the bird and also keeps it moist during baking (they are usually not eaten). Legs need not be tied.

Renaissance

Generously sprinkle salt, ground black pepper and dried thyme on the breast and back of the duck and place on a rack in a deep baking pan. The pan needs to be deep in order to catch all the fat. The rack needs to lift the duck above the fat.

Place in a preheated 450-500° oven for 1/2 hour. Reduce temperature to 400° and bake an additional 1-1/2 to 2 hours (times are approximate and are for 1 - 2 five pound ducks.) The duck should be a deep golden brown; the skin will be very crisp and most of the fat cooked off.

Sauce:
In a saucepan melt 3 Tbsp. butter. Sauté 2 shallots and 2 cloves of garlic minced fine until soft. Whisk in 3 Tbsp. flour. Cook a little. Add 1 Tbsp. tomato paste, 2 tsp. kitchen bouquet (a browning ingredient - not essential for flavor), 1-1/2 cups chicken broth, 1 cup port, 1-1/2 cups Renaissance Cabernet Sauvignon, 2 -3 Tbsp. green peppercorns (packed in water), black pepper and salt.

Let this come to a boil. Sauté it down to a simmer allow to reduce by one third. Add about 1/2 cup cream, then taste for balance. Add more salt, pepper, wine, etc., as necessary.

Extra sauce will keep and is also good over steaks.

CA' DEL SOLO
PRUNUS

Grappa and Wine Marinated Cornish Game Hen

1 C. Ca del Solo Malvasia Bianca
3 cloves garlic, diced
1/4 C. olive oil

1/4 C. Ca del Solo Prunus (Eau de Vie)
1 T. fresh thyme, finely chopped
4 Cornish Game Hens

Combine wine, eau de vie, garlic, thyme and oil (salt and pepper to taste). Rinse the game hens dry with a paper towel, butterfly (remove bones) and add to liquid. Marinate overnight. Grill for five minutes, brush with marinate and turn, grill for and additional five minutes or until done.

LOUIS M. MARTINI WINERY
GEWURZTRAMINER

Roasted Cornish Game Hens

Stuffing:
1 C. long grain rice
1/2 t. salt
1/4 t. ground cinnamon
1 t. freshly grated orange rind
1/2 C. chopped pecans

2 C. chicken stock
1 T. butter
1/4 t. ground cardamon
1/2 C. chopped pitted dates

6 Cornish Game Hens
6 T. butter, softened
1/4 C. Louis M. Martini Gewurztraminer

salt, pepper
1/2 C. orange marmalade

Bring chicken stock, salt, butter, cinnamon, cardamon, orange rind to a boil. Add rice, cover and reduce heat. Simmer 20 minutes and let sit 5 minutes. Fluff with a fork and stir in dates and pecans. Preheat over to 350°.

Rinse hens and pat dry. Salt and pepper cavity and stuff with 1/2 cup of rice mixture. Secure legs with string and place hens in a roasting pan. Brush the hens with softened butter and roast for 30 minutes. Melt orange marmalade with white wine and reduce slightly. Raise oven to 400°, baste hens with marmalade mixture and continue roasting an additional 20-30 minutes or until juices run clear and hens are browned. Baste occasionally with the marmalade mixture, and if the hens start to darken to much, cover with foil.

HEITZ CELLARS
CABERNET SAUVIGNON

Barbequed Leg of Lamb
By Rollie Heitz

1 butterflyed leg of lamb
several large sprigs of rosemary

Marinade:

1 bottle Heitz Cellars Grignolino   10-15 cloves crushed garlic
1 T. fresh ginger, finely chopped   1 t. fresh ground black pepper
1 T. curry power   3 T. dijon style mustard
3/4 C. honey   2 t. cumin
1 t. ground allspice   2 T. rosemary leaves *

Combine all marinade ingredients in a large saucepan and heat on low for 20 minutes. Remove marinade from heat and pour over lamb in a large bowl or deep roasting pan. Place in refrigerator turning lamb every 1/2 hour. Marinate for at least 4 hours, overnight is best. Grill lamb on hot coals turning every four or five minutes until done. Add sprigs of rosemary to fire as lamb is cooking. Best served with Heitz Cellar Cabernet Sauvignon.

BUENA VISTA
PINOT NOIR

Carneros Lamb

3 lb. leg of lamb   1 C. Buena Vista Carneros Pinot Noir
1 C. light soy sauce   1/2 C. olive oil
1/4 C. coarse mustard   zest of lemon
handful of rosemary and mint   handful of oregano
1 t. sea salt   1 T. cracked pepper

Have the butcher butterfly a leg of lamb, making sure that the thickest parts are no more than 2" thick. If using fresh herbs, coarsely chop (or cut the herbs with scissors) into 1" chunks. Put the ingredients of the marinade in a large bowl. Place the lamb in the bowl fat side up, so that the meat is in contact with the juices. Refrigerate; marinate for at lease 4 hours, preferably overnight. Strain and reserve the marinade. Reduce over high heat while the lamb is cooking. Grill the lamb over a hot fire, turning several times, until done but still pink. Let rest 15 minutes before carving. Add any meat juices to the reduced marinade.

SHAFER VINEYARDS
CABERNET SAUVIGNON

Encrusted Rack of Lamb

1 Rack of lamb, 8 chops (frenched), prepared by butcher
1/4 C. Lamb scraps, from above (no fat)
1/4 C. Leek bottom, fine chop
1 small Carrot, fine dice
1 stalk Celery, fine dice
1/2 medium Onion, fine dice
1 T. Shallot, fine dice
1 T. Oil
1 C. Rich beef broth
1/2 C. Red wine
4 slices Sourdough breadcrumbs, coarse
Pecans, toasted, chopped coarse
1/4 C. breadcrumb
1 sprig Rosemary, fresh
1 t. Pepper, fresh cracked
3 T. Dijon mustard
1 Egg yolk
1 t. Honey
1/2 t. Rosemary, fresh, fine chop
Salt and pepper to taste
1 T. Butter, unsalted

Season rack and sear. Place in roasting pan and into a 350° oven for 45 - 50 minutes or until there is an internal temperature of 130°- 135°.

Degrease pan and sauté vegetables and lamb trimmings. Deglaze with red wine and reduce to marmalade state. Add rosemary sprig and stock, reduce by half. Season and whisk in cold butter. Mix mustard, egg yolk, honey and fine chopped rosemary in a bowl. On a plate mix breadcrumbs and pecans. Remove lamb from oven and allow to cool slightly.

Generously brush mustard mixture on flesh side and press on breadcrumb mixture. Place rack back into oven and allow crust to brown. Internal temperature should be 140°. Remove from oven and allow to set 5 - 10 minutes before carving.

Serve with Gratin of Potato and Wild Rice (see index) and seasonal vegetables.

SEGHESIO WINERY
PINOT NOIR

Glazed Lamb Chops
Serves 6

6 lamb loin chops, 3/4 to 1 inch thick
2 T. Orange Blossom honey
1-2 T. Seghesio Pinot Noir

Freshly ground pepper
2 T. Dijon Mustard

Trim excess fat from each chop. Score the fat edge with a knife to prevent curling while broiling. Place the chops on a broiler pan. Sprinkle each chop with pepper. In a bowl, combine the honey, mustard and wine for a glaze. Brush top side of each chop with the glaze mixture. Broil for 4 minutes. Turn chops over, brush the second side with glaze and broil for 3 to 4 minutes longer. Be careful not to overcook the meat. Serve with a glass of Seghesio Pinot Noir.

DRY CREEK VINEYARDS
MERLOT

Grilled Lamb Kabobs
By Brad Wallace

1/2 C. olive oil
1/3 C. red wine vinegar
2 T. dijon mustard
1/2 t. allspice
1/4 t. cayenne pepper
1 t. salt
2 T. fresh rosemary, minced

1/4 C. Dry Creek Merlot
3 large cloves garlic, minced
1/2 C. minced onion
1/4 t. nutmeg
1 T. fresh ground pepper
1 t. sugar
2 lb. boneless lamb, cut into 2-inch cubes

3 large red bell peppers, seeded and cut into equal squares
2 Japanese eggplants, stem removed, sliced equally
skewers

Combine first 13 ingredients in a non-corrosive bowl; mix well. Add cubed lamb and vegetables, toss well. Marinate 30-45 minutes, or longer if you need. Thread bell pepper, eggplant, and lamb alternately on the skewers, ending with vegetables. Grill on both sides until brown, but still pink on the inside; approximately 8 minutes total. Serves six. Enjoy with Dry Creek Vineyards Merlot.

CLOS PEGASE
CABERNET SAUVIGNON

Lamb Chops with Vegetables and Fruits

6-6 oz. lamb chops
3 kiwi, peeled and scooped into balls
2 C. seedless red or green grapes
24 asparagus spears, trimmed and sliced diagonally
2 thin cucumbers, peeled and scooped into balls
1/3 C. each, fresh parsley and mint, minced

Preheat oven to 350°. Arrange each chop on a piece of foil season to taste with salt and pepper. Scatter fruits and vegetables around chops, dividing equally. Sprinkle herbs over all. Seal the foil packets, and set on a baking sheet. Bake for 20 minutes for medium rare. Transfer packets to individual serving dishes. Serve with Clos Pegase Cabernet Sauvignon.

FROG'S LEAP
MERLOT

Rack of Lamb

3-4 Racks of lean lamb
4 oz. grated Asiago cheese
4 cloves garlic
2-3 T. mustard

1/3 C. roasted hazel nuts, chopped
1/8 C. fresh minced thyme
Sea salt, pepper to taste
1/3 C. extra virgin olive oil

In a food processor, add hazelnuts, Asiago cheese, thyme, garlic and mustard to form a paste. Slowly add olive oil until well incorporated into paste and cover each lamb rack equally with the mixture.

In a hot, oven-proof skillet, sear the racks in a small amount of olive oil to brown. Remove the racks and deglaze the pan with 1/2 cup Merlot or Cabernet Sauvignon. Reduce the liquid to a sauce, decant to a small pan and replace the lamb. Roast in a 400° oven for about 20 minutes. Lamb should still be pink when served with the warm sauce. The fruit and soft tannin of a Merlot is a delicious complement to this meal. Serve simply, accompanied by roasted new potatoes and a steamed vegetable or tossed salad.

97

ALEXANDER VALLEY VINEYARDS ZINFANDEL

Green Chili Pozole

3 lbs. Boneless pork loin
2 - 15 oz. cans hominy
2 - 8 oz. cans Hernandez salsa verde (a pureed mixture of tomatillo's, cilantro and serrano peppers. Other brands will suffice.)
2 t. Cumin
1 t. garlic, minced
1 t. Italian Spice mix
1 large can whole green chilies, rinsed and chopped medium
1 - 15 oz. can beef stock
1/4 C. cilantro, finely chopped
Spike season mix (substitute salt if unavailable)
pepper
olive oil

Cut pork into one-inch cubes, spike liberally with spike and pepper. Refrigerate for about one hour.

Brown garlic in olive oil (do not burn) and then brown pork quickly. Do not over cook. Remove pork from skillet to a crockpot or 6-1/2 quart saucepan with a tight fitting lid. Drain hominy and add to pot with beef stock, salsa verde, chilies, and spices. Simmer over low heat until pork is tender. (In a crockpot, this takes 4-5 hours; on the stove top it may take less time but you may need to add additional stock or water.) Do not cook on too high a heat.

Delicious served with a side of black beans, tortilla's, and chopped avocado. A tossed green salad sprinkled with toasted pumpkin seeds and citrus dressing compliments the dish nicely; a don't forget a glass of Alexander Valley Vineyards Zinfandel.

PINE RIDGE
CHARDONNAY

Honey Roasted Pork
Serves 6

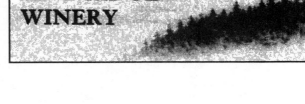

3 cloves garlic, peeled
1/4 C. fresh parsley, chopped
1 t. fresh thyme, leaves only
1 T. olive oil
3 T. honey
salt
1 C. dry white wine
1 5-7 lb. boneless pork loin, rolled and tied
black pepper to taste
1 small onion, finely chopped
2 cloves garlic, peeled and smashed
1 C. tomato sauce, preferably homemade
1 T. unsalted butter

In the bowl of a food processor fitted with a steel blade OR a blender, process the 3 cloves garlic, parsley, thyme, olive oil, honey, 1 tsp. salt, and 1 Tbsp. wine into a smooth paste.

With a sharp knife, make small slits in the meat. Force generous quantities of the paste into the slits. Rub the remaining mixture all over the pork. Put the pork in a large roasting pan and pour in the remaining wine. Cover and marinate unrefrigerated for several hours (or refrigerate overnight, turning the meat several times).

Preheat oven to 400°. Drain off and reserve the wine. Sprinkle the top of the roast with salt and pepper and bake for 10 - 15 minutes. Lower the oven temperature to 325° and cook for approximately 2 hours more or until a meat thermometer reads 185° (approximately 35 minutes per pound). Transfer the pork to a heated serving platter, remove the string, and keep the roast warm.

Pour off all but 2 Tbsp. of fat from the roasting pan. Add the onion and remaining garlic and sauté gently for 2 to 3 minutes. Add the reserved wine to pan and stir over heat. Add the tomato sauce and cook until reduced to half. Remove the heat and swirl in the butter. Correct the seasoning with salt and pepper. Carve the pork into thin slices and serve with spoonfuls of the sauce.

ZACA MESA
JOHANNISBERG RIESLING

Loud Mouth Stuffed Pork Chops

8 - 1 inch pork chops

l egg
1/2 t. thyme or fresh
3 golden delicious apples in 1/2 inch cubes
1 C. celery
1 C. onion
2 C. diced french bread in 1/2 inch cubes
1/2 C. dried french cherries
1/2 C. Zaca Mesa Johannisberg Riesling
4 T. butter
3 T. maple syrup
1/2 C. roasted chili pecans
chicken stock, if needed

Put butter in sauté pan add thyme, celery, onion and apples. Sauté for 5 minutes, add 1/2 cup of Riesling, cook until onion and apples are soft, about 10-15 minutes. Add salt and pepper.

Put pecans in dish, pour Riesling over and let marinade for 2 hours. Take out of wine and toss in medium spice chili powder mix. Put in 350° oven for 15-20 minutes.

Put stuffing mix with roasted chili pecans and dry bread cubes and mix. Add maple syrup and chicken stock until bread cubes are moist, add egg. Stuff pork chops with stuffing (chops are sliced and stuffed to the point it looks like an open mouth), pour leftover wine from the marinated pecans and bake in 350° oven for 30-40 minutes. Don't over cook.

SANFORD WINERY
SAUVIGNON BLANC

Sesame-Lime Pork Medallions

Created especially By Shirley Sarvis, good accompaniments are steamed white rice; and plums, melon or persimmons for dessert. You can be generous in adding topping-seasonings; add them to taste.

1 fresh pork tenderloin, completely trimmed of fat, and of an even thickness (narrow end trimmed off for another use), about 1/2 pound meat
Salt
2 t. unsalted butter
1 T. freshly grated fresh lime peel
1/16 t. ground hot red pepper (cayenne)
1-1/2 T. warm melted unsalted butter
1 T. lightly toasted sesame seeds
36 fresh cilantro leaves (no stems) (about 3 tablespoons)
Slender lime wedges

Wipe meat dry. Season surfaces well with salt. Let stand for 1 hour. Heat the 2 teaspoons butter in a medium-sized heavy frying pan over medium heat until it bubbles. Add meat and cook, slowly turning, until richly browned on all sides and a little pink near center, about 17 to 18 minutes total. Remove from pan and let stand for 5 minutes. Carve crosswise into scant 1/2 inch thick slices. Arrange, slightly over-lapping, on warm serving plates; season well with salt. Sprinkle with lime peel. Add red pepper to melted butter and spoon over. Sprinkle with seeds. Sprinkle cilantro alongside. Garnish with lime wedges and squeeze on juice to taste. Makes 2 servings.

Note: Use ample butter in browning meat; you want the browning to be deep and a little crisped.

Make a small cut to test pork doneness; cook to slightly less doneness than you will want at time of serving; consider that pork will continue cooking as it rests before carving.

To toast sesame seeds:
Sprinkle in a single layer on a shallow baking sheet. Bake in a 325° oven until light golden, only about 3 to 5 minutes; shake occasionally.

SANFORD WINERY
PINOT NOIR

SANFORD

Pancetta Quail
Created especially by Shirley Sarvis

Salt and freshly ground pepper
1 t. shallots, finely minced
1/2 C. Sanford Pinot Noir
2 oz. very thinly sliced pancetta
1 T. unsalted butter
1-1/2 C. lean chicken or quail stock
4 whole boneless breasts of fresh plump quails

1 T. unsalted butter, melted and cooled
1/2 T. unsalted butter
1/4 t. crumbled dried thyme
1/2 T. soft unsalted butter
1 T. soft unsalted butter in small pieces

16 very thin slices (about 1/8 inch thick) small baguette slices from excellent French bread (non-sour), crusts removed

Wipe breasts dry. Split each whole breast in half; cut each split breast piece in half, lengthwise. Season pieces very well with salt and pepper. Turn in the 1 tablespoon melted butter to cloak. Let stand at room temperature for about 30 minutes.

In a shallow pan, sauté shallots in the 1/2 tablespoon butter just to heat and cloak with butter. Add stock, wine and thyme and cook over high heat until liquid is reduced to about 1/2 cup. Trim baguette slices to 1 1/4 inch diameter size; lightly toast to be golden on both sides and crisp throughout.

Cook pancetta in a frying pan until tender and cooked through, but not crisp nor browned. Spread toast pieces generously with the 1/2 tablespoon soft butter, then top with pancetta to cover and extend slightly over toast edge. Arrange on serving tray. Heat the 1 tablespoon butter in a medium-sized or large heavy frying pan over medium heat until it bubbles. Add breast pieces and sauté until nicely lightly browned on both sides, just done (as soon as rosy color disappears in center), and very moist and tender and juicy, about 3 minutes total (do not crowd in pan; add a little more butter if necessary in order to keep quail very well buttered).

Remove and place each on top of a toast pancetta piece. Remove from the sauté pan the liquid butter drippings; leave golden brown crusty drippings. Add the reduced wine stock mixture. Cook and stir until reduced to a generous 1/4 cup. Remove from heat and wisk in the 1 tablespoon soft butter pieces to give a creamy finish. Season very well with salt and pepper. Spoon over each quail piece as guest wishes an appetizer. Garnish serving tray with fresh thyme sprigs if you wish.

KENWOOD VINEYARDS ZINFANDEL

Salsicce alla vin Zin Sauce

1/4 C. best quality olive oil
6 Italian sausages
6 large cloves garlic, chopped
1 medium onion, chopped
2-8 oz. cans tomatoes, undrained
2 t. dried oregano
1 6-inch cinnamon stick (broken in half)
salt and fresh ground pepper to taste
1/2 C. Kenwood Vineyard Sonoma Zinfandel

KENWOOD

1 5-1/2 oz. can tomato paste
2 t. dried basil
1/4 t. hot red pepper flakes

Heat oil in large saucepan. Add sausages and fry until browned, about 10 minutes. Drain and set aside. In the same pan add garlic and onions and cook until onions are tender, about 4 minutes. Add remaining ingredients. Lower heat and simmer for 30 to 40 minutes. Add sausage and simmer for another one to three hours, stirring occasionally. Serve over hot pasta, with grated parmesan cheese and pepper to taste. Serve with Kenwood Sonoma Valley Zinfandel.

BYINGTON WINERY PINOT NOIR

Escalopes de Veau au Chanterelle

2 oz. Chanterelle mushrooms
2 C. Cream
2 T. demi-glace
2 T. shallots
1/2 C. flour
1/2 C. brandy
2 oz. clarified butter
2 lbs. Veal Rib Eye (sliced 1" thick, then pounded to 1/4")

BYINGTON

Dip pounded veal in flour. Sauté in clarified butter (rare). Set aside, but leave warm. In pan, put shallots and deglaze with cognac. Add demi-glace and mushrooms and cream. Reduce until thick. Pour over the veal. Serve with Byington Pinot Noir.

103

FICKLIN VINEYARDS
TINTA PORT

Ficklin Port Marinated Roast Loin of Veal
This unusual method calls for marinating the loin and placing the tenderloin inside it.
Serves 6.

2 to 3 lb. loin and tenderloin of veal
1 bottle Ficklin Tinta Port
3 medium oranges, juiced with zest finely chopped
1 C. coarsely chopped fresh basil
1 T. ground black pepper
Salt to taste
1 cup veal or chicken stock

Trim the loin of all fat and sinew. In a deep roasting pan combine wine, orange juice and
zest, basil, pepper, and salt. Add the loin, cover and marinate in the refrigerator for 24 hours.

Preheat the oven to 350°. Remove the loin from the marinade, make a cut three-fourths
through the width of the loin, spread out, and place the tenderloin in the center of the loin.
Close to form a cylinder and tie securely with kitchen string.

Roast the meat on a rack until a meat thermometer inserted in the center of the roast registers
between 135° to 140°, about 1-1/4 hours. Let rest for ten minutes under a loose foil tent.

While the roast is in the oven, strain three cups of the marinade into a non-reactive pan. Boil
over high heat until reduced to 1-1/2
cups, about twenty minutes. Add the
stock and cook over medium-high heat
until sauce is reduced to about 1 cup
and is slightly thickened, about 12 minutes. Add the pepper and salt to taste if
necessary. Reheat, if necessary, before
serving.

FICKLIN
Vineyards
MADERA
CALIFORNIA

To serve, slice roast about 1/2 inch
thick and drizzle sauce over all.

CHALK HILL WINERY
CABERNET SAUVIGNON

CHALK HILL
WINERY

Porcini Veal Stew

1 oz. Porcini mushrooms
1 C. all-purpose flour
1 T. pepper
1 bay leaf
3 lbs. lean veal stew meat
1 onion, chopped
1 can beef broth
12 boiler onions

1 C. water
1 T. salt
1 T. cumin
1/4 C. olive oil
6 garlic cloves
12 oz. fresh mushrooms
1 C. Chalk Hill Cabernet Sauvignon
1/2 C. chopped parsley

Combine porcini and water in sauce pan and bring to boil; set aside. Combine dry ingredients and dredge meat in mixture; brown meat in olive oil in dutch oven. Remove meat and add onions, garlic and fresh mushrooms, sauté. Add Chalk Hill wine, beef broth, browned meat, onions and parsley. Bake in oven for 1-1/2 hours. Serves six.

SANFORD WINERY
PINOT NOIR-VIN GRIS

SANFORD

Vin Gris Veal Chops

Created especially by Shirley Sarvis. You might accompany with a small swirl of buttered fine flat paste (such as tagliarini or tagliatelle) alongside (buttered and seasoned with salt and black pepper); and buttered fresh spinach, or a mild leaf lettuce salad after the veal.

salt and freshly ground black pepper
1 T. grated fresh lemon peel
8 small or 4 large one-inch-thick rib or loin chops

5 T. unsalted butter
1/2 C. Sanford Vin Gris

Wipe chops dry. Season well with salt and pepper. Let stand for 1 hour. Heat butter in a heavy very large frying pan over medium heat until it bubbles well (use two pans to avoid crowding chops if necessary). Add chops and brown on one side; turn and brown on second side; turn once more, cooking until tender and slightly pink near bone, about 12 minutes. Remove to warm serving plates. Sprinkle with lemon peel. Add wine and cook while stirring over high heat until juices are blended and reduced to a thin consistency, about 4 Tbsp. Spoon over chops. Serves 4.

LOUIS M. MARTINI WINERY CHARDONNAY

Clam Pasta

2 T. butter
1-2 cloves garlic, minced
10 oz. Whole baby clams
salt & white pepper to taste
2 lbs freshly steamed clams (optional)

2 T. flour
1-1/2 C. half & half
1/4 t. thyme
8 oz. dried paste, cooked
parmesan cheese

Drain clams and reserve liquid. In a medium sauce pan melt butter and sauté garlic briefly. Do not allow color. Add flour and cook for 2 minutes. Whisk in half & half, reserve clam juice and cook until sauce thickens. Season with thyme, salt and freshly ground pepper. Remove sauce from heat and add clams. Cook pasta and toss with the sauce. Garnish with steamed clams, if desired. Serve with Parmesan cheese and a glass of Louis M. Martini Chardonnay.

SEGHESIO WINERY ZINFANDEL

Lasagna with Besciamella Sauce
Serves 10 - 12

2 pork chops
6 Italian Country sausages
3 cloves garlic, mashed
2 T. fresh parsley, minced
2 - 8-oz cans tomato sauce
1/2 C. white wine

1-1/2 lbs. ground beef
1 medium onion, chopped
1 stalk celery, chopped
Salt, pepper, thyme and sage
1 large can whole tomatoes, strained
2 C. water

Brown pork chops in oil. Remove and brown ground beef. Return pork chops to pan and add onion, celery and garlic. Sauté all these ingredients together. Add minced parsley, salt, pepper, thyme and sage. Add tomato sauce, tomatoes, wine and water and simmer slowly for 1-1/2 hours.

Besciamella Sauce:
3 T. butter
2 C. milk
Salt and Pepper

5 T. flour
1 C. whipping cream
Dash of nutmeg   *Continued...*

In heavy sauce pan, melt butter, stir in flour and cook, stirring constantly, until paste cooks and bubbles a bit, but don't let it brown (about 2 minutes). Add the hot cream and milk, continuing to stir, as the sauce thickens, about 2 to 3 minutes. Bring to boil and remove from heat. Add salt, pepper and a dash of nutmeg to taste.

Remove the casing from Italian country sausages, break up and brown in a separate skillet. Place these in your sauce for the last 25 minutes of cooking time. Cook 1 - 8oz. package of lasagna until al dente and rinse under cold water. Lay out on towels to dry.

Remove the pork chops from the sauce and put several tablespoons of the red sauce in the bottom of an 11 x 7 inch casserole. Lay strips of lasagna over the sauce, then put sauce over them and spoon besciamella sauce on and sprinkle with Romano cheese. Repeat the same layering, finishing with cheese. Serve with French rolls and a salad. Serve this dish with a Seghesio Reserve Zinfandel. May be served the same day or refrigerated overnight. If refrigerated, heat in a 350° oven for 40 minutes.

SUTTER HOME ZINFANDEL

Pasta with Italian Sausage & Zinfandel

SUTTER HOME

2 T. olive oil
2 cloves garlic, minced or pressed
1/4 t. whole fennel seeds, crushed
1 C. pasta sauce
1/2 C. grated parmesan cheese
1 lb. hot (or mild) Italian sausage, casings removed
1 large green bell pepper, seeded and chopped coarsely

1 large onion, chopped coarsely
2 T. dry basil
1/2 C. Sutter Home Zinfandel
1/4 C. chopped Italian parsley
12 oz. dry pasta

In a wide frying pan over medium heat, crumble sausage. Cool, stirring often until meat is well browned. Remove from heat and discard all excess fat. Transfer meat to a small bowl. Over medium heat, add 1 Tbsp. olive oil, onions, bell pepper, garlic, basil, and fennel. Stir often with a spatula, lifting browned bits from the bottom of pan. Continue to cook until onion is translucent, about 5 minutes. Return sausage to pan and add wine. Bring to a boil, scrape in all flavor bits from bottom of pan. Add pasta sauce and simmer 5 minutes. Cook pasta in 4 quarts of boiling water until tender (8-10 minutes). Drain well.

In a warm, large serving platter, combine parsley and the remaining tablespoon of olive oil. Add pasta and mix lightly using two forks. Pour sauce over. Makes 4 servings. Garnish with Parmesan cheese, serve with a tossed salad, crusty bread and Sutter Home Zinfandel.

MCDOWELL VALLEY VINEYARDS
FUME' BLANC

Pasta with Scallops in Lemon Herb-Cream Sauce

1/2 C. butter
1/2 C. McDowell Fume Blanc
1 C. clove garlic, minced
2 shallots, finely minced
2 C. cream
1 T. lemon zest
1/2 lb. scallops
2 t. fresh marjoram, chopped
2-4 oz. Pasta per person

Wash, dry and chop fresh herb (marjoram, fennel, tarragon or basil). Melt butter in non-corrosive saucepan and sauté garlic and shallots for two minutes or until golden brown. Add scallops and sauté, coating with butter. Add wine and poach for 3-5 minutes. Take care not to over cook or the scallops will toughen.

Remove scallops and keep warm. Reduce liquid by one-third. Add cream, reduce for twenty minutes: however, during the last five minutes, add fresh herbs and lemon zest, and stir until warmed through. Fold in scallops.

While sauce is reducing, cook pasta until "just" done. Drain and rinse quickly with warm water. Shake out excess water. Coat with 1-2 tablespoons of olive oil. Toss pasta with sauce and garnish with fresh herbs, lemon zest or chopped red and yellow pepper and fresh cracked pepper.

Developed by Richard Keehn, Proprietor, McDowell Valley Vineyards

108

CHALK HILL WINERY
SAUVIGNON BLANC

CHALK HILL
WINERY

Pasta with Shrimp, Asparagus and Cream Sauce

1 lb. pasta
4 T. olive oil
1 lb. asparagus
1 C. Chalk Hill Sauvignon Blanc
3 T. arrowroot
Cilantro

4 T. butter
3 cloves garlic, crushed
1 lb. medium shrimp
1-1/2 C. whipping cream
salt and pepper

Boil water with 2 Tbsp. of olive oil and salt. Cook pasta. Wash and drain shrimp; sauté in 2 Tbsp. butter. Add asparagus and steam about 2 minutes, set aside. Heat butter and remaining oil and sauté garlic. Add Chalk Hill wine and when it has evaporated, add cream and arrowroot and whisk until thickened, correct salt and pepper. In a large bowl, toss drained pasta, shrimp and asparagus with sauce and sprinkle with chopped cilantro. Serves 6.

SEGHESIO WINERY
ZINFANDEL

SEGHESIO
SINCE 1902

Penne Puttanesca

1/4 C. olive oil
1 whole garlic head, chopped
1 - 28 oz. can diced tomatoes
7 anchovy fillets, coarsely chopped

1 onion, chopped
1/2 t. red pepper flakes
12 Kalamatar olives, pitted and chopped
2 T. drained capers

Sauté onion, garlic and pepper flakes in olive oil. Put tomatoes in a blender and puree, then add to sautéed ingredients. Cook approximately 45 minutes to one hour. Simmer slowly. Remove from heat and add remaining ingredients. Spoon over freshly cooked and drained Penne Rigate, Mostaccioli or Spiral Pasta. Add grated Parmesan or Romano Cheese.

This is a recipe that I enjoyed preparing and serving to our guests this past summer. It is very tasty.

THE HESS COLLECTION
CABERNET SAUVIGNON

Saffron Pasta Fettuccini with Duck Confit, Crimini Mushrooms and Sun Dried Tomatoes
By Bill Briwa

Pasta:
2 C. bread flour
2 C. semolina flour
2 C. durham flour
6 eggs
1/3 C. olive oil
2 T. salt
1/3 cup water
3/4 t. saffron threads

Combine the saffron and hot water and allow to steep for 20 minutes. Put all the flours together into a mixer bowl with eggs, olive oil, and mix thoroughly. Add saffron water a little at a time until the paste dough comes together into a ball. Knead the dough for 8 minutes with a dough hook. Allow the dough to rest at room temperature for 1 hour. With a pasta machine roll the pasta to the thinnest setting and then cut into the desired shape. Cook pasta in a large pot of salted, boiling water until tender, about 3 minutes.

Sauce:

2 T. olive oil	1/4 onion, minced
1 clove garlic, minced	1/3 lb. Crimini mushrooms, sliced thick
2 C. veal stock	2 C. duck stock
2 T. parsley, chopped	1 t. thyme, chopped
1-1/2 t. capers, chopped	1 C. duck confit, shredded
1/4 sun dried tomatoes, cut into thin strips	2 T. nicoise olives
1/4 parmesan cheese, grated	Black ground pepper

Reduce the stock by 1/2. Sauté the mushrooms, onions and garlic in the oil. Add the duck, tomatoes, olives, herbs and reduced stock to the mushroom mixture. Adjust consistency (if needed) by stirring in a small piece of beurre maine and allowing the sauce to return to a boil. Salt and pepper to taste. Serve the sauce over cooked saffron pasta and sprinkle with chopped parsley, grated cheese and cracked black pepper. Serve with The Hess Collection Cabernet Sauvignon.

CLOS PEGASE CHARDONNAY

CLOS PEGASE

Won Ton Ravioli with Paprika Cream

1/2 C. minced shallots or onion	2 t. each olive oil and butter or margarine
1/2 C. whipping cream	2 T. lemon juice
2-3 T. water	1/2 t. paprika
Won tons (directions follow)	Thin leek or green onion slices

In a 10- to 12-inch frying pan over medium-high heat, frequently stir shallots with oil and butter until limp, about 5 minutes. Add cream, lemon juice, 2 tablespoons water and paprika. Stir until bubbling; set aside and keep warm.

Meanwhile, bring 2 quarts of water to boiling in a 4 to 5 quart pan. Add won tons and cook on high heat, uncovered, until dough is tender to bite, about 2 minutes. Thin sauce to original consistency, with water if needed; spoon equally onto 4 warm plates. With a slotted spoon, lift out won tons; put 3 on each plate. Garnish with leeks and paprika.

Won Tons:
Lay 12 won ton skins flat. In center of each, mound equal portions of 1/4 cup shredded Jack cheese and two tablespoons minced leeks. Rub rims with a paste of 1 tablespoon EACH all-purpose flour and water. Fold won tons over filling, aligning edges and pressing seal. If made ahead, cover and chill up to 8 hours.

111

CAKEBREAD CELLARS
CABERNET SAUVIGNON

Pizza with Roast Eggplant, Peppers, Red Onions & Fresh Herbs

Dough:

2-1/2 C. all-purpose unbleached flour	2 C. semolina flour
1 T. yeast	1 t. salt
1 T. olive oil	1-1/2 C. warm water

Mix the first 5 ingredients together in an electric mixer with a dough hook. Add water and continue mixing until dough forms a ball. Remove from work bowl and knead on a floured surface until dough is soft and elastic. Place in a greased bowl covered with plastic wrap and allow to rise until double in size, about one hour. Punch dough down and portion into 6 balls. Store on a floured sheet tray covered with plastic wrap in the refrigerator.

Filling:

2 medium Italian eggplant	3 roasted red peppers, diced
1 medium red onion, chopped	3 cloves garlic, minced
2 T. olive oil	1 lb. provolone, grated
1 C. parmesan, grated	1 T. rosemary
1 T. oregano	2 T. parsley

Pierce eggplants with a fork, place on a sheet tray and roast in a preheated 450° oven until soft, about 20-25 minutes. Remove from oven and set aside until cool enough to handle. At that point, peel the skin off and cut into a medium dice. In a large sauté pan, sauté the onion and garlic in the olive oil until soft. Add the eggplant and peppers and cook through. Season with salt and pepper. Remove from heat and reserve.

To prepare pizzas, take a piece of dough from the refrigerator and flatten on a floured work surface. Work dough out to the edges using your fingertips, into a round about 9 - 12 inches. Top with a couple spoonfuls of eggplant mixture, spread thinly over the top. Sprinkle with a small handful of provolone cheese and parmesan and dust with fresh herbs. Bake in a preheated 500° oven until crisp and browned on top, about 10-15 minutes. Cut into slices and enjoy with a glass of Cakebread Cellars Cabernet Sauvignon.

Note: Pizzas are best baked directly on a pizza stone, which can be found at many gourmet food stores or they can also be baked on sheet trays dusted with cornmeal, placed in the middle of the oven. The dough won't be quite as crisp and will take slightly longer but should still turn out well.

DESSERTS

RENAISSANCE VINEYARDS
LATE HARVEST RIESLING

Almond Biscotti

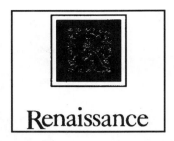

Renaissance

1 3/4 C. flour
1/2 t. baking soda
1/2 t. baking powder
1/8 t. Salt
1/2 C. unsalted butter   1 C. sugar
2 lg. eggs   2 t. grated orange peel
1-1/2 t. vanilla extract   1/4 t. almond extract
1-1/2 C. almonds, lightly toasted and coarsely chopped

Sift first flour ingredients into medium sized bowl. Using electric mixer, cream butter in another bowl until light. Gradually add sugar and beat until fluffy. Mix in the eggs one at a time. Mix in orange peel and vanilla and almond extracts. Mix in walnuts. Add dry ingredients and refrigerate until well chilled. (Can be prepared one day ahead or more.)

Preheat oven to 350°. Butter and flour two baking sheets or use parchment paper. Divide dough into 3 pieces. Using lightly floured hands, roll each into 1-1/2" wide long pieces on a lightly floured surface. Arrange two logs on one sheet, spacing 5" apart. Arrange third log on second sheet. (Logs spread during baking). Bake until logs are light brown, about 20 minutes. Cool slightly on pan. Cut logs on baking sheet crosswise on diagonal into 3/4" wide slices. Turn cut side down on sheet and bake until golden brown, about 15 minutes. Allow to cool. Perfect with Renaissance Special Select Late Harvest Riesling!

CLOS PEGASE
CABERNET SAUVIGNON

Almond Chocolate Cake

4-1/4 oz. Butter
2-1/2 T. flour
120 grams sugar
125 grams unsweetened chocolate
4 eggs
1/2 T. baking powder
100 grams powdered almond

Preheat oven to 325 °. Melt chocolate and butter. Mix 3 egg yolks and 1 whole egg with sugar (save 3 whites for melange.) Add powdered almond to egg mixture and blend well. Add melted chocolate, butter, flour, and baking powder. Make melange with 3 egg whites and mix with the above. Place in mold and bake at 325° for 30 minutes or so.

MIRASSOU
BLANC DE NOIRS CHAMPAGNE

Brandied Cranberry Pinwheel with Chantilly Cream

Brandied Cranberry Filling:
1-12 oz. package fresh (or Frozen) cranberries
1 C. sugar
1/2 C. brandy, divided

In a saucepan, combine cranberries, sugar, and 1/2 cup brandy. Bring to a boil. Reduce heat and boil gently for 10 minutes, stirring occasionally. Remove from heat. Stir in remaining 1/4 cup brandy. Cool before using.

Cake:
5 egg yolks   5 oz. almond paste, softened
2/3 C. sugar, divided   5 egg whites
1/2 C. flour, sifted   1-1/2 C. heavy cream
powered sugar for garnish and Chantilly Cream

Place egg yolks, almond paste, and 1/3 cup sugar in bowl of electric mixer. Beat at high speed until mixture is smooth and becomes pale yellow in color. In another bowl, whip the egg whites with the remaining 1/3 cup sugar to a medium-soft peak. Fold whites into yolk mixture. When whites have incorporated halfway, fold in flour.

Butter a jelly roll pan (15-1/2" X 10" X 1") and line with buttered parchment paper. Spread cake mixture evenly in pan. Bake in pre-heated 500° oven for 5 minutes, until slightly browned. Cool cake in pan. Run knife around sides of pan to loosen cake. Spread cranberry filling thinly and evenly over cake. (You will have more filling than you need for this.) Roll cake into a pinwheel, removing parchment paper as you roll. Place cake seam side down on serving plate and sprinkle with powered sugar.

Chantilly Cream:
Whip heavy cream, sweetening to taste with powered sugar.

To serve, cut cake into slices and pass bowl of Chantilly Cream or, using a pastry bag, pipe a boarder of cream around each slice on individual serving plates. Serve with Mirassou Blanc de Noirs Champagne.

FICKLIN VINEYARDS
TINTA PORT

Chocolate Cake with Chocolate Sauce

This is a confection of chocolate sauce on dense-chocolate brownie-like wedges. It is a delicious and exotic dessert, with intense chocolate flavors in harmony with the spirit and vibrancy of Ficklin's port wine. Serves 12.

1/2 C. unsalted butter
2 large eggs
1/4 t. salt
2 oz. (2 squares) unsweetened baking chocolate
1/2 C. chopped walnuts (optional)
Port chocolate sauce (recipe below)

1 C. sugar
1/2 t. vanilla
1/2 C. sifted all-purpose flour

Coarsely chop chocolate squares. Heat butter in a heavy saucepan over medium-low heat until half melted. Add chocolate and stir with a wooden spoon until chocolate and butter are melted and blended. Remove from heat. Stir in sugar, stirring until dissolved. Add eggs, one at a time, and beat with spoon after each addition until mixture is thoroughly combined and shiny. Stir in vanilla and salt. Stir in flour. Turn into a buttered 9-inch round layer cake pan and spread smooth. Bake in a 350° oven until slightly firm to touch and toothpick inserted in center shows mixture is a little moist, about 25 minutes. Let cool in pan on a rack. To serve: Cut into wedges and top each with warm sauce.

Ficklin Port Chocolate Sauce:

Combine in top part of double boiler over hot (not boiling) water 1 package (4 oz) sweet baking chocolate, coarsely chopped, and 1/2 cup Ficklin Tinta Port. Heat and whisk until smooth. Makes about 1 cup, or topping for 6 to 8 dessert servings.

Note: *The sauce is the consistency of syrup. It is an excellent topping for vanilla ice cream, egg-white butter cake or pound cake.*

CA' DEL SOLO
GRAPPA DI MALVASIA

Chocolate Grappa Cake

1/2 C. raisins
3/4 C. + 1 T. all-purpose flour
9 oz. fine-quality bittersweet or semi-sweet chocolate, chopped
1 stick (1/2 C.) unsalted butter, cut into pieces
6 large eggs, separated
1/2 C. sugar
1/3 C. grappa di Niagara or Muscato
1 t. vanilla
1/3 C. pine nuts
confectioners' sugar for dusting the cake
whipped cream as an accompaniment, if desired

Grappa di Moscato
GRAPPA BRANDY

In a small bowl let the raisins soak in warm water to cover for 20 minutes. Drain the raisins, pat them dry between paper towels, and in a small bowl toss them with 1 tablespoon of flour until they are coated. Line the bottom of a buttered 9-inch springform pan with a round of wax paper, butter the paper, dust the pan with flour, knock out the excess.

In a metal bowl, set over a pan of barely simmering water, melt the chocolate with the butter, stirring occasionally, until the mixture is smooth, remove the bowl from the heat, and let the mixture cool for 5 minutes. In a large bowl, whisk together well the egg yolks, the granulated sugar, the grappa, and the vanilla and stir in the chocolate mixture, a spoonful at a time, stirring well after each addition. Add the remaining 1/4 cup of flour, stirring until the batter is just combined, and fold in the raisins and the pine nuts.

In another large bowl, with an electric mixer beat the egg whites with a pinch of salt until they just hold soft peaks, stir one fourth of them into the batter and fold in the remaining whites gently but thoroughly.

Turn the batter into the prepared pan, smooth the top, and bake the cake in the middle of pre-heated 350° oven for 40 to 50 minutes, or until it is puffed and small cracks appear on the top. (The center will be slightly moist.) Let the cake cool in the pan on a rack for 10 minutes, remove the side and bottom of the pan and the wax paper, and let the cake cool completely on the rack. Dust the cake lightly with the confectioners' sugar and serve it with whipping cream.

PINE RIDGE
MERLOT

Gateau Nancy
Serves 8

3-1/2 oz. sweet butter
1/2 T. ground almonds
5 egg whites
7 oz semi-sweet dark chocolate, crumbled
1 T. Grand Marnier OR 1/2 T. orange extract

1/2 t. vanilla extract
5 egg yolks
3/4 C. sugar

In a metal bowl, put all ingredients except eggs and sugar. Melt over a pot of boiling water, removing from heat. Whisk ingredients together lightly. Whip egg yolks and half of the sugar until white ribbon is formed, about 5-7 minutes. Blend into chocolate mixture with rubber spatula. Whip egg whites vigorously, slowly adding sugar until stiff peaks form. Fold gently into chocolate mixture careful to not deflate whipped egg whites.

Line a 10" springform pan with parchment paper (heavy waxed paper available in supermarket next to plastic wrap and foils). Butter and flour inside of pan. Pour in batter gently. Bake in pre-heated 275° oven for one hour and twenty minutes. During baking process, do not open oven door. Remove from oven when toothpick inserted in center, comes out clean. When testing cake for doneness, open oven door gently.

Serve slices of cake sprinkled with powdered sugar and creme anglaise***.

***Creme Anglaise:*
(Makes 2-1/2 cups)
2 cups milk
4 egg yolks, room temperature
1/2 cup sugar

Heat milk in heavy saucepan until a "skin" forms. Remove from heat. Beat the egg yolks and sugar in a mixer bowl until thick and light. Gradually beat in the milk. Pour back into the saucepan and cook, stirring constantly, over low heat until the mixture coats the back of a wooden spoon (This can take as long as 15 minutes.). DO NOT LET BOIL as milk will curdle!

Remove pan from the heat and place mixture in clean mixing bowl set in ice water to cool to room temperature.

PINE RIDGE
CHARDONNAY

Olive Oil Cake
Serves 6

5 eggs plus 2 egg whites
1 T. mixed grated orange and lemon peel
1/2 t. salt
1/2 C. plus 2 T. extra virgin olive oil

3/4 C. sugar
1 C. sifted flour
1/2 C. good quality dessert wine

Preheat oven to 375°. Separate the 5 eggs and beat the egg yolks with 3/4 cup sugar in a bowl with a whisk for 3 to 5 minutes until light-colored and well-beaten. Add the orange and lemon peel and set aside.

Combine 1 cup sifted flour and 1/2 tsp. salt, and then add, bit by bit, to the sugar and egg mixture, beating continually until it is incorporated. Add the dessert wine and the olive oil in the same fashion. Beat the 7 egg whites until they stand in stiff peaks, and then fold them into the mixture thoroughly.

Pour this batter into an 8-inch spring-form pan whose bottom has been lined with parchment paper and whose entire interior is well buttered. Bake for 20 minutes, rotating the cake if necessary to ensure even cooking. After 20 minutes, lower the oven temperature to 325° and bake for another 20 minutes. Then turn off the oven and leave the cake in the closed oven for 10 minutes more while the cake deflates. Remove the cake from the oven, invert it onto a flat surface, remove the spring form pan, and allow it to cool completely.

***Creme Anglaise:**
(Makes 2-1/2 cups)
2 C. milk
4 egg yolks, room temperature
1/2 C. sugar

Heat milk in heavy saucepan until a "skin" forms. Remove from heat.

Beat the egg yolks and sugar in a mixer bowl until thick and light. Gradually beat in the milk. Pour back into the saucepan and cook, stirring constantly, over low heat until the mixture coats the back of a wooden spoon (This can take as long as 15 minutes.) DO NOT LET BOIL as milk will curdle! Remove pan from the heat and place mixture in clean mixing bowl set in ice water to cool to room temperature.

CLOS PEGASE
RESERVE CABERNET SAUVIGNON

Turkish Chocolate Delight

2 oz. Nuts
6 oz. Biscuit
7 oz. Butter
9 oz. Black Chocolate
2 Whole Eggs

Directions: Chop walnuts, small fingernail size. Crack biscuits (simple dry biscuits) to thumb fingernail size. Melt black chocolate and butter together and add two whole eggs, roughly beaten in advance. Add nuts and biscuits and optionally two tablespoons of cognac and/or orange rind.

CUVAISON
CABERNET SAUVIGNON

Valrhona Bittersweet Chocolate Fondue with Strawberries

1/2 lb. Valrhona bittersweet chocolate, grated
1 C. water
1 t. cinnamon
1/2 t. nutmeg, freshly grated

Using a double boiler, melt the chocolate completely. Add cinnamon and nutmeg, stirring to incorporate completely. Keep warm in fondue pot and serve with fresh strawberries.

Serve with Cuvaison Cabernet Sauvignon.

PIPER SONOMA
METHODE CHAMPENOISE-BRUT

Sparkling Sabayon

Special thanks to John Ash of Aqua Restaurant in San Francisco for this stunning sparkling Sabayon recipe.

7 large egg yolks	1/2 C. sugar
pinch of salt	1 C. Piper Sonoma Brut
2 T. kirsch	

Beat the yolks, sugar and salt until light. Place mixture in top of a double boiler and whisk in the wine and kirsch. Place over simmering water and whisk until mixture mounds and quadruples in volume. Serve immediately (warm) with fresh fruits and berries and with Cookies Florentine

Cookies Florentine:

1/2 C. butter	1/2 C. light corn syrup
1/2 C. sugar	1 C. walnuts, chopped
1/2 C. flour	1 T. lemon rind

Combine butter, corn syrup and sugar in a saucepan. Place over low heat, stirring frequently, until warm. Blend in walnuts and flour. Add lemon rind. On greased cookie sheet, make circles (4" in diameter) using approx. 2 Tbsp. of dough per circle. Bake at 350° for about 10 minutes or until golden brown. Cool slightly. Roll circles around the handle of wooden spoon to form tubes. Allow to cool completely and harden before serving.

EBERLE WINERY
MUSCAT CANELLI

California Cream

Serve over your favorite fruit with a glass of Eberle Muscat Canelli for a simple and refreshing summer dessert.

8 ounces cream cheese
1 C. sour cream
1 C. whipping cream
1 egg yolk
2 T. sugar or honey

Blend above ingredients together in a blender. Sweeten to taste and pour over fresh fruit and berries.

ALEXANDER VALLEY VINEYARDS
MERLOT

Almond Macaroons

1 - 8 oz. can almond paste
pinch of salt
1/4 t. almond extract
1/2 C. butter, softened
pine nuts for decoration

2 extra large egg whites
1 C. sugar
2 T. grated almonds
baking parchment paper

Preheat oven to 325°. Break up almond paste into small chunks and place in food processor. Add egg whites, salt, sugar, almond extract and almonds. Blend until smooth. Generously butter parchment paper and place on a large cookie sheet. Drop the cookie mixture onto the paper by teaspoon. Flatten tops with a knife dipped in water and place 3 or 4 pine nuts on each cookie. Bake for 20 minutes. Remove paper to a rack to cool, then carefully peel paper from cookies. If the cookies are difficult to remove, try moistening back of paper with water. These macaroons are best when served the same day; however they freeze well.

123

RENAISSANCE VINEYARDS
LATE HARVEST SAUVIGNON BLANC

Pear Pie

Renaissance

Crust:
In a cuisinart combine:
1-3/4 c. flour
5 oz. sweet butter
1/4 c. sugar

Start to blend, then add:
2 egg yolks
1/4 tsp. vanilla
(a little water if dough is too dry)

Remove dough and knead slightly to finish mixing. Press evenly into a 10" pie pan. Chill until ready to bake.

Filling:
1 C. sugar
6 T. flour
3 eggs
3/4 C. melted sweet butter
2 t. vanilla

In a bowl, mix above five ingredients. Peel, core and slice thin, crosswise, 3 ripe pears. (Yellow Bartlett pears are good). Place pears, fanned out in a decorative pattern on the pie crust. Pour the filling over the pears and bake in a preheated 325°oven. Bake about one hour, checking after 40 minutes. Cover loosely with foil if crust is browning too quickly. Bake until set.

Serve with Renaissance Late Harvest Sauvignon Blanc.

KORBEL
CHAMPAGNE/BRUT

Strawberry Sweetheart Pie
By Teresa Douglas-Mitchell, Culinary Director

4 C. Strawberries, sliced
3 T. Korbel Brut Champagne
3 T. Flour
2 T. powdered sugar (for dusting)

1 C. Sugar
1/2 t. Freshly ground nutmeg
2 Eggs, beaten

Roll out the cookie dough (chill for 20-30 minutes first) into a 12-13 inch circle. Press into a removable bottom 10" tart pan, a heart shaped pan, or individual tart molds, saving the scraps. Chill again.

Combine gently the strawberries and other ingredients. Pour this mixture into the lined pan/pans. Bake at 400° for 35 to 40 minutes or until set (less for smaller pans).

Cool for 20 minutes, then dust with powdered sugar.

Note: For a great Valentine's Day presentation, roll out the scrap dough and cut into heart shapes. Decorate the top of the pie before baking.

EBERLE WINERY
MUSCAT CANELLI

Raspberry Delamain
Serves 8

2 pints fresh raspberries
2 T. honey
Juice of 1/2 lemon
2 T. cognac, preferable Delamain
Sweetened whipped cream

Wash and rinse raspberries and place in bowl. Combine honey, lemon juice and cognac and pour over berries. Refrigerate 1 hour or longer. Spoon into glasses; top with whipped cream.

KORBEL
CHAMPAGNE/BRUT

Champagne Shortbread
By Teresa Douglas-Mitchell, Culinary Director

16 T. Butter (2 sticks)
2/3 C. Confectioners Sugar
1 T. Korbel Brut Champagne
2 C. Flour
1/4 t. Salt

Chop butter into small pieces, and place in a food processor. Add the sugar and champagne. Sift the dry ingredients over these. Blend until a soft round ball of dough is formed.

Chill the dough, until firm but workable. Roll out on a floured surface to 1/4 - 3/8 inch thick. Cut into shapes or press into a shortbread mold.

Bake on an ungreased cookie sheet at 350° for approximately 20 minutes. (They shouldn't brown!) Cool and dust with granulated or confectioners sugar. Makes 24 cookies

Note: For chocolate shortbread cookies, add 1/2 cup unsweetened Cocoa to the dry ingredients, but reduce the flour to 1-3/4 cups .

RODNEY STRONG VINEYARDS
SAUVIGNON BLANC

German Strawberry Shortcake
Recipe courtesy of Charlotte Strong

Two-egg Cake:
1/3 C. Butter
1 C. Sugar
2 eggs, unbeaten
1 t. Vanilla
2 C. Sifted cake flour
3 t. Baking powder
1/2 t. Salt
2/3 C. Milk

Cream butter. Add sugar slowly. Beat well, adding eggs one at a time. Add vanilla. Sift flour, baking powder, and salt together and add alternately with milk to creamed mixture. Bake in a greased 9x5x3" pan at 350° for 1 hour. (A fluted cake pan makes this dessert even prettier!)

Fresh Strawberry Topping:
1 qt. Fresh Strawberries
3/4 C. Sugar
1-1/2 T. Cornstarch
dash Salt
1 t. Butter
1 C. Water
2 t. Fresh lemon juice
1/4 t. Vanilla

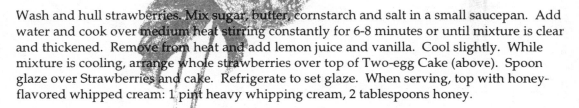

Wash and hull strawberries. Mix sugar, butter, cornstarch and salt in a small saucepan. Add water and cook over medium heat stirring constantly for 6-8 minutes or until mixture is clear and thickened. Remove from heat and add lemon juice and vanilla. Cool slightly. While mixture is cooling, arrange whole strawberries over top of Two-egg Cake (above). Spoon glaze over Strawberries and cake. Refrigerate to set glaze. When serving, top with honey-flavored whipped cream: 1 pint heavy whipping cream, 2 tablespoons honey.

KORBEL
CHAMPAGNE/BRUT

Champagne Cream
By Teresa Douglas-Mitchell, Culinary Director

1 t. Unflavored Gelatin
1 /8 C. Korbel Brut Champagne
1 /2 C. heavy cream   1 /4 C. Sugar
1 /2 C. sour cream   1 /2 t. Vanilla
1 C. Fresh Strawberries, Raspberries, etc.   1 T. Sugar
1 t. Balsamic Vinegar

Soften the gelatin in the champagne. Add the cream and sugar, then place in a small saucepan. Heat briefly and gently until all is dissolved. Set aside.

Whip the sour cream and vanilla together. Slowly add the warm cream, beating consistently. Pour into a 1 - 2 cup mold (or 2 individual molds), and refrigerate a couple of hours until the cream is chilled and set. Serve with fresh berries, flavored with the balsamic vinegar and sugar.

EBERLE WINERY
MUSCAT CANELLI

Strawberries in Muscat Orange Sauce

2 C. sweet Muscat wine   1/2 C. orange marmalade
1/3 C. sugar, or less, only if necessary   1 Valencia or other juice orange
1 T. Contreau or other orange liqueur   1 t. vanilla extract
3 baskets (1 pint each) fresh strawberries

Make the sauce in advance so it may be cooled before serving. In a non-reactive saucepan, combine the wine and marmalade. Bring to boil and let simmer for 10 minutes, or until the mixture thickens to the consistency of a light syrup. Remove the pan from heat and allow the sauce to cool. Peel and section the orange using the following method: Cut the top and bottom from the orange. Stand the orange on a cutting board and cut the peel away. Holding the orange over a bowl to catch the juices, cut out wedges, using the section membranes as a guide. Add the juices to the warm sauce. Reserve the sections to add at the last minute. When the sauce is cool, add the liqueur and vanilla and stir in the orange sections. Rinse berries and pat them dry. Stem and cut the berries into slices or chunks. Sprinkle them with about 1 tablespoon of sugar and set them aside for up to one hour before serving. Pour the sauce over the berries just before serving.

CLOS PEGASE
MERLOT

Strawberry Foam
Serves 4

2-1/2 C. sliced strawberries (reserve a few whole ones for garnish)
2 t. unflavored gelatin
1/2 C. water
sugar to taste

In a food processor or blender, puree 2-1/2 cups sliced strawberries; add sugar to taste. In a 1- to 2-cup pan, mix 1 envelope (2 teaspoons) unflavored gelatin with 1/2 cup water; let stand until liquid is absorbed, then stir over medium heat until melted. Whirl into strawberries. Pour mixture into a bowl; cover and chill until thickened but not firm, about 30 minutes.

With a mixer, beat mixture until foamy; pour into a 4 by 8 inch pan (or individual bowls). Cover; chill until firm 2 hours, or wait until the next day. To unmold, dip pan in hot water until edges barely melt; invert into plate. Cut in 4 pieces; put in bowls. Garnish with whole strawberries.

HUSCH VINEYARDS
GEWURZTRAMINER

Zabaglione

5 egg yolks
1/2 C. sugar
1/2 Husch Gewurztraminer
1 C. heavy cream

Beat the egg yolks, sugar and Gewurztraminer over hot water in a double boiler until light and thick. Remover from heat and keep beating (with an electric blender until cool). Whip a cup of heavy cream and fold it into cooled mix. Spoon over sliced strawberries or kiwi in stern glasses. Serves 4-6 depending on the amount of fruit.

129

FOREST HILL VINEYARDS CHARDONNAY

One, Two, Three Apple Tart

Crust:
1/2 C. butter
1 C. sugar
1-1/4 C. all-purpose flour
1/2 t. salt
1/2 t. cinnamon
1/4 t. baking powder

Filling:
4 Pippin or Granny Smith apples, peeled, cored, quartered and sliced in thin crescents
1 egg well-mixed
1 C. heavy cream

Cream butter and sugar until fluffy in food Processor. Add the rest of the dry ingredients and cut into cornmeal consistency—six to seven on-off turns ONLY or you'll overdo it. Reserve 1/3 C. of this mixture.

With finger tips, press dough into 11-inch removable bottom tart pan. Arrange fruit in swirls. Sprinkle with 1/3 C. reserved crust mixture and bake in pre-heated 375° oven for 15 minutes. Pour egg-cream mixture over fruit. Bake 25 minutes longer.

Serve with Forest Hill Chardonnay.

IRON HORSE VINEYARDS
PINOT NOIR

Prune Tart

Tart dough:
1-1/2 C. all-purpose flour
Pinch salt
1-1/2 sticks of sweet butter (room temperature)
3 T. water

In a mixing bowl combine flour and salt; add butter in small cubes using the tips of your fingers (cold hands are better) until the mixture resembles coarse meal.

Add the butter one tablespoon at a time to make a soft dough. Place in refrigerator to chill and roll on a lightly floured surface to form a 10-1/2 inch circle. Place the dough in a 10 inch tart shell and gently press in place; trim excess dough.

Filling:
3 C. pitted prunes	1 C. powdered sugar
1/4 C. flour	1/2 C. heavy cream
1/2 C. fig jam	1-1/2 sticks butter, salted
3 eggs	1-1/2 C. almonds
1 t. orange flower water	

Place prunes in bowl and cover with hot water until they plump up; drain and set aside. In large mixing bowl mix the butter and sugar, and beat until well blended. Add the eggs one at a time, along with flour, almonds, cream and orange flower water. Pour the mixture into the tart shell; arrange the prunes on top.

Cooking:
Preheat oven to 375°. Bake for 40 minutes; remove from oven and brush with fig jam. Slice into six pieces and serve with creme franzcie.

Wine Notes: The last drop of wine in the glass will be delicious with this dessert. Pinot Noir and prunes have a natural affinity. Both are black fruits and Pinot Noirs often take on a "pruney" personality.

131

Appendix A

CONTENTS BY WINE

CHENIN BLANC

GEWURZTRAMINER

GRAPPA

118	CA' DEL SOLO	Chocolate Grappa Cake
3	BONNY DOON VINEYARDS	Grappa Marinated Goat Cheese
93	CA' DEL SOLO	Grappa and Wine Marinated Cornish Game Hen

RIESLING

12	RENAISSANCE VINEYARDS	Scallop Quenelles
100	ZACA MESA	Loud Mouth Stuffed Pork Chops
114	RENAISSANCE VINEYARDS	Almond Biscotti

MELON

80	J. FRITZ WINERY	Chicken Dijon with Cracked Pepper & Herb Sauce

MERLOT

123	ALEXANDER VALLEY VINEYARDS	Almond Macaroons
53	ALEXANDER VALLEY VINEYARDS	Vegetables a la Murphy
129	CLOS PEGASE	Strawberry Foam
70	CUVAISON	Curried Crepes filled with Sea Bass and Rock Prawns
96	DRY CREEK VINEYARDS	Grilled Lamb Kabobs
97	FROG'S LEAP	Rack of Lamb
119	PINE RIDGE	Gateau Nancy
3	PINE RIDGE	Grilled Eggplant and Cheese Appetizer
46	PINE RIDGE	Grilled Vegetable and Frisee Salad

PINOT NOIR-VIN GRIS

41   SANFORD WINERY
       Coriander Duck Salad
35   SANFORD WINERY
       Herb Vegetable Beef Soup
1   SANFORD WINERY
       Lemon Sun Tomatoes Crostini
45   SANFORD WINERY
       Spinach-Capellini Salad
105   SANFORD WINERY
       Vin Gris Veal Chops

SANGIOVESE

33   SEGHESIO WINERY
       Minestone

SAUVIGNON BLANC

9   BUENA VISTA
       Old Fashioned Crab Cakes
16   CAKEBREAD CELLARS
       Satay with Peanut Sauce
56   CAKEBREAD CELLARS
       Singapore Satay Sauce
109   CHALK HILL WINERY
       Pasta with Shrimp, Asparagus and Cream Sauce
63   CLOS PEGASE
       Sea Bass a la Pegasus
26   FROG'S LEAP
       Prawn Bar-b-que
30   GROTH VINEYARDS & WINERY
       Corn Chowder with Cumin and Red Pepper
4   GROTH VINEYARDS & WINERY
       Pesto Cheese Hors d'oeuvre
36   GROTH VINEYARDS & WINERY
       Zucchini Soup
90   MURPHY-GOODE WINERY
       Thai Grilled Chicken
64   QUIVIRA VINEYARDS
       Grilled Salmon, Japanese Style

LATE HARVEST SAUVIGNON BLANC

SYRAH

61 MC DOWELL VALLEY VINEYARDS
Red Wine with Fish

PORT

117 FICKLIN VINEYARDS
Chocolate Cake with Chocolate Sauce
40 FICKLIN VINEYARDS
Cranberry Port Melange
104 FICKLIN VINEYARDS
Ficklin Port Marinated Roast Loin of Veal

WHITE ZINFANDEL

14 BANDIERA
Spicy Apricot-Ginger Appetizer
85 OAK RIDGE VINEYARDS
Roast Chicken Royal
4 SUTTER HOME
Onion & Cheese Appetizers with White Zinfandel

ZINFANDEL

98 ALEXANDER VALLEY VINEYARDS
Green Chili Pozole
78 CAKEBREAD CELLARS
Wild Boar Ribs with Robert's Secret Barbecue Sauce
103 KENWOOD VINEYARDS
Salsicce alla vin Zin Sauce
61 SEGHESIO WINERY
Chili Beans
106 SEGHESIO WINERY
Lasagna with Besciamella Sauce
109 SEGHESIO WINERY
Penne Puttanesca
56 SEGHESIO WINERY
Red Sauce
107 SUTTER HOME
Pasta with Italian Sausage & Zinfandel

Appendix B

CONTENTS BY WINERY

118	CA' DEL SOLO Chocolate Grappa Cake	GRAPPA DI MALVASIA
18	CAIN CELLARS Moroccan Squab Pie	CAIN FIVE
34	CAIN CELLARS Chestnut Soup	CAIN FIVE
5	CAKEBREAD CELLARS Suppli Telephono	CHARDONNAY
7	CAKEBREAD CELLARS Miniature Crab Cakes with Homemade Tartar Sauce	CHARDONNAY
16	CAKEBREAD CELLARS Satay with Peanut Sauce	SAUVIGNON BLANC
19	CAKEBREAD CELLARS Cheese Puffs with Wild Mushrooms & Leeks	CHARDONNAY
27	CAKEBREAD CELLARS Smoked Trout, Watercress, Pears and Fresh Dill on Belgian Endive Spears	CHARDONNAY
56	CAKEBREAD CELLARS Singapore Satay Sauce	SAUVIGNON BLANC
78	CAKEBREAD CELLARS Wild Boar Ribs with Robert's Secret Barbecue Sauce	ZINFANDEL
112	CAKEBREAD CELLARS Pizza with Roast Eggplant, Peppers, Red Onions & Fresh Herbs	CABERNET SAUVIGNON
81	CHALK HILL WINERY Chicken with Tomatoes and White Wine Sauce	CHARDONNAY
105	CHALK HILL WINERY Porcini Veal Stew	CABERNET SAUVIGNON
109	CHALK HILL WINERY Pasta with Shrimp, Asparagus and Cream Sauce	SAUVIGNON BLANC
38	CLOS PEGASE Cheese Mousse	CHARDONNAY
44	CLOS PEGASE Shrimp and Crab Mold	CHARDONNAY
46	CLOS PEGASE Chilled Tofu Timbale with Chives	CHARDONNAY
63	CLOS PEGASE Sea Bass a la Pegasus	SAUVIGNON BLANC
78	CLOS PEGASE Tataki Fillet	CABERNET SAUVIGNON
97	CLOS PEGASE Lamb Chops with Vegetables and Fruits	CABERNET SAUVIGNON

117	FICKLIN VINEYARDS	TINTA PORT
	Chocolate Cake with Chocolate Sauce	
69	FOREST HILL VINEYARD	CHARDONNAY
	Sunshine Scallops	
130	FOREST HILL VINEYARDS	CHARDONNAY
	One, Two, Three Apple Tart	
26	FROG'S LEAP	SAUVIGNON BLANC
	Prawn Bar-b-que	
87	FROG'S LEAP	CHARDONNAY
	Roasted Chicken	
97	FROG'S LEAP	MERLOT
	Rack of Lamb	
4	GROTH VINEYARDS & WINERY	SAUVIGNON BLANC
	Pesto Cheese Hors d'oeuvre	
20	GROTH VINEYARDS & WINERY	CHARDONNAY
	Stuffed White Mushrooms in Phyllo	
30	GROTH VINEYARDS & WINERY	SAUVIGNON BLANC
	Corn Chowder with Cumin and Red Pepper	
36	GROTH VINEYARDS & WINERY	SAUVIGNON BLANC
	Zucchini Soup	
74	GROTH VINEYARDS & WINERY	CABERNET SAUVIGNON
	Filets with Groth Cabernet	
64	HANNA WINERY	CHARDONNAY
	Grilled Salmon Steaks & Pineapple Salsa	
77	HANNA WINERY	CABERNET SAUVIGNON
	Steak & Mushrooms a' la Hanna	
69	HEITZ CELLAR	CHARDONNAY
	Citrus & Apricot Prawns	
94	HEITZ CELLARS	CABERNET SAUVIGNON
	Barbequed Leg of Lamb	
110	THE HESS COLLECTION	CABERNET SAUVIGNON
	Saffron Pasta Fettuccini with Duck Confit, Crimini Mushrooms and Sun Dried Tomatoes	
29	HUSCH VINEYARDS	PINOT NOIR
	Portuguese Soup	
68	HUSCH VINEYARDS	CHARDONNAY
	Scallops with Papaya and Ginger Beurre Blanc	
129	HUSCH VINEYARDS	GEWURZTRAMINER
	Zabaglione	
17	IRON HORSE VINEYARDS	FUME BLANC
	Rabbit Sausage	

32	IRON HORSE VINEYARDS	WEDDING CUVEE CHAMPAGNE
	Cream of Green Lentil Soup	
40	IRON HORSE VINEYARDS	PINOT NOIR
	Pear & Pomegranate Salad	
86	IRON HORSE VINEYARDS	PINOT NOIR
	Roast Chicken with Lemon and Olives	
131	IRON HORSE VINEYARDS	PINOT NOIR
	Prune Tart	
80	J. FRITZ WINERY	MELON
	Chicken Dijon with Cracked Pepper & Herb Sauce	
1	KENWOOD VINEYARDS	CABERNET SAUVIGNON
	Sun Dried Tomato Crostini with Asiago Cheese	
103	KENWOOD VINEYARDS	ZINFANDEL
	Salsicce alla vin Zin Sauce	
66	KORBEL	CHAMPAGNE/BRUT
	Poached Salmon with Five Minute Sauces	
125	KORBEL	CHAMPAGNE/BRUT
	Strawberry Sweetheart Pie	
126	KORBEL	CHAMPAGNE/BRUT
	Champagne Shortbread	
128	KORBEL	CHAMPAGNE/BRUT
	Champagne Cream	
93	LOUIS M. MARTINI WINERY	GEWURZTRAMINER
	Roasted Cornish Game Hens	
106	LOUIS M. MARTINI WINERY	CHARDONNAY
	Clam Pasta	
61	MC DOWELL VALLEY VINEYARDS	SYRAH
	Red Wine with Fish	
108	MC DOWELL VALLEY VINEYARDS	FUME' BLANC
	Pasta with Scallops in Lemon Herb-Cream Sauce	
11	MIRASSOU	AU NATUREL CHAMPAGNE
	Oyster Flan with Fennel Fumet	
89	MIRASSOU	BRUT CHAMPAGNE
	Steamed Chicken Breasts Stuffed with Red Pepper Mousse in Champagne Sauce	
116	MIRASSOU	BLANC. DE NOIRS CHAMPAGNE
	Brandied Cranberry Pinwheel with Chantilly Cream	
75	MURPHY-GOODE WINERY	CABERNET SAUVIGNON
	Irish Stew	
90	MURPHY-GOODE WINERY	SAUVIGNON BLANC
	Thai Grilled Chicken	

29	OAK RIDGE VINEYARDS	FUME BLANC
	Bean Soup	
51	OAK RIDGE VINEYARDS	CHARDONNAY
	Savory Rice Pilaf	
85	OAK RIDGE VINEYARDS	WHITE ZINFANDEL
	Roast Chicken Royal	
67	PEDRONCELLI	FUME BLANC
	Seared Salmon with Rice Paper & a Citrus Vinaigrette	
3	PINE RIDGE	MERLOT
	Grilled Eggplant and Cheese Appetizer	
15	PINE RIDGE	CHARDONNAY
	Chicken Skewers	
23	PINE RIDGE	CHARDONNAY
	Skewered Tortellini	
25	PINE RIDGE	CHENIN BLANC
	Phyllo Spring Rolls	
39	PINE RIDGE	CHARDONNAY
	Tarragon-Orange Vinaigrette	
46	PINE RIDGE	MERLOT
	Grilled Vegetable and Frisee Salad	
49	PINE RIDGE	CHARDONNAY
	Lacy Potato Pancakes	
55	PINE RIDGE	CHENIN BLANC
	Pickled Ginger Sauce	
57	PINE RIDGE	CHENIN BLANC
	Soy-Ginger Glaze	
59	PINE RIDGE	CHENIN BLANC
	Wasabi Sauce	
59	PINE RIDGE	CHENIN BLANC
	Yellow Bell Pepper Sauce	
88	PINE RIDGE	CHENIN BLANC
	Sa-Teh on Skewers	
99	PINE RIDGE	CHARDONNAY
	Honey Roasted Pork	
119	PINE RIDGE	MERLOT
	Gateau Nancy	
120	PINE RIDGE	CHARDONNAY
	Olive Oil Cake	
58	PIPER SONOMA	METHODE CHAMPENOISE-BLANC DE NOIRS
	Sparkling Citrus Marinade for Chicken or Seafood	

122	PIPER SONOMA	METHODE CHAMPENOISE-BRUT
	Sparkling Sabayon	
39	QUIVIRA VINEYARDS	CHARDONNAY
	Avocado and Melon Salad	
64	QUIVIRA VINEYARDS	SAUVIGNON BLANC
	Grilled Salmon, Japanese Style	
80	QUIVIRA VINEYARDS	CABERNET SAUVIGNON
	Balinese Chicken	
12	RENAISSANCE VINEYARDS	DRY RIESLING
	Scallop Quenelles	
63	RENAISSANCE VINEYARDS	SAUVIGNON BLANC
	Pasta with Lobster Sauce	
79	RENAISSANCE VINEYARDS	CABERNET SAUVIGNON
	Arroz con Pollo	
92	RENAISSANCE VINEYARDS	CABERNET SAUVIGNON
	Roast Duckling with Green Peppercorn Sauce	
114	RENAISSANCE VINEYARDS	LATE HARVEST RIESLING
	Almond Biscotti	
124	RENAISSANCE VINEYARDS	LATE HARVEST SAUVIGNON BLANC
	Pear Pie	
2	RODNEY STRONG VINEYARDS	PINOT NOIR
	Chever Cheese & Roasted Walnuts	
35	RODNEY STRONG VINEYARDS	SAUVIGNON BLANC
	Chilled Curried Zucchini Soup	
43	RODNEY STRONG VINEYARDS	CHARDONNAY
	Orzo & Artichoke Salad	
127	RODNEY STRONG VINEYARDS	SAUVIGNON BLANC
	German Strawberry Shortcake	
1	SANFORD WINERY	PINOT NOIR-VIN GRIS
	Lemon Sun Tomatoes Crostini	
8	SANFORD WINERY	CHARDONNAY
	Chervil Lobster in Lettuce	
9	SANFORD WINERY	SAUVIGNON BLANC
	Lemon Chive Halibut	
10	SANFORD WINERY	CHARDONNAY
	Cloved Lobster-Butter Canapes	
10	SANFORD WINERY	CHARDONNAY
	Lemon Pepper Lobster	
14	SANFORD WINERY	PINOT NOIR
	Beef Fillet on Mushrooms	

16	SANFORD WINERY	SAUVIGNON BLANC
	Sage Prosciutto Pork	
21	SANFORD WINERY	CHARDONNAY
	Pistachio Clove Butter	
22	SANFORD WINERY	CHARDONNAY
	Lemon-Cream-Wine Capellini	
35	SANFORD WINERY	PINOT NOIR-VIN GRIS
	Herb Vegetable Beef Soup	
41	SANFORD WINERY	PINOT NOIR-VIN GRIS
	Coriander Duck Salad	
45	SANFORD WINERY	PINOT NOIR-VIN GRIS
	Spinach-Capellini Salad	
75	SANFORD WINERY	PINOT NOIR
	New York Steak Arugula	
82	SANFORD WINERY	SAUVIGNON BLANC
	Cumin Chicken with Green Olive Salsa	
90	SANFORD WINERY	PINOT NOIR
	Dijon Duck Breasts	
101	SANFORD WINERY	SAUVIGNON BLANC
	Sesame-Lime Pork Medallions	
102	SANFORD WINERY	PINOT NOIR
	Pancetta Quail	
105	SANFORD WINERY	PINOT NOIR-VIN GRIS
	Vin Gris Veal Chops	
34	SEBASTIANI VINEYARDS	CHARDONNAY
	Quick Minestrone	
6	SEGHESIO WINERY	SAUVIGNON BLANC
	Torte	
26	SEGHESIO WINERY	CABERNET SAUVIGNON
	Italian Sausage Stuffed Mushrooms	
33	SEGHESIO WINERY	SANGIOVESE
	Minestone	
50	SEGHESIO WINERY	CHARDONNAY
	Risotto	
51	SEGHESIO WINERY	CHARDONNAY
	Risotto Milanese	
56	SEGHESIO WINERY	ZINFANDEL
	Red Sauce	
61	SEGHESIO WINERY	ZINFANDEL
	Chili Beans	

84	SEGHESIO WINERY	SAUVIGNON BLANC
	Italian Chicken	
96	SEGHESIO WINERY	PINOT NOIR
	Glazed Lamb Chops	
106	SEGHESIO WINERY	ZINFANDEL
	Lasagna with Besciamella Sauce	
109	SEGHESIO WINERY	ZINFANDEL
	Penne Puttanesca	
48	SHAFER VINEYARDS	CABERNET SAUVIGNON
	Gratin of Potato and Wild Rice	
73	SHAFER VINEYARDS	CHARDONNAY
	Walnut Encrusted Trout	
95	SHAFER VINEYARDS	CABERNET SAUVIGNON
	Encrusted Rack of Lamb	
22	ST CLEMENT	MERLOT
	Grilled Oysters with Pink Butter	
41	ST CLEMENT	SAUVIGNON BLANC
	Fiesta Winter Salad	
49	ST. SUPERY	SAUVIGNON BLANC
	Lemon Risotto	
74	ST. SUPERY	CABERNET SAUVIGNON
	Flank Steak Extraordinaire	
4	SUTTER HOME	WHITE ZINFANDEL
	Onion & Cheese Appetizers with White Zinfandel	
30	SUTTER HOME	CHARDONNAY
	Fish Market Cioppino with Chardonnay	
38	SUTTER HOME	CHENIN BLANC
	Chicken Salad with Chenin Blanc	
107	SUTTER HOME	ZINFANDEL
	Pasta with Italian Sausage & Zinfandel	
100	ZACA MESA	JOHANNISBERG RIESLING
	Loud Mouth Stuffed Pork Chops	